THE
PATH TO FREEDOM

THE
PATH TO FREEDOM

by
Michael Collins

Foreword by
Tim Pat Coogan

Roberts Rinehart Publishers

Published in the US and Canada by Roberts Rinehart Publishers,
5455 Spine Road, Boulder, Colorado 80301

Distributed by Publishers Group West

Foreward © 1996 Tim Pat Coogan
Text © 1996 Roberts Rinehart Publishers

Published in Ireland by Mercier Press

Library of Congress Catalog Card No 95-72790

ISBN 1-57098-064-0

Typesetting:
Red Barn Publishing, Skeagh, Skibbereen, Co. Cork, Ireland

CONTENTS

FOREWORD

America's loss was to be Ireland's gain. For if
Michael Collins had taken his brother Pat's
advice, the Republic of Ireland might not
exist today. Watching the storm clouds of World War
I gather over Europe, Pat had written to Michael from
Chicago urging his young brother to leave his job in
a London financial institution and come to join him
in America. Had they teamed up, one is tempted to
speculate that one of the all-time great Pat-and-Mike
success stories might have resulted. As it was, Pat
became a captain of police in Chicago and Michael
went on to destroy the Irish police force, the armed
Royal Irish Constabulary (R.I.C.). In doing so he laid
the foundations for today's unarmed Irish police, the
Garda Síochána or Civic Guard.

In the early stages of World War I, the then twenty-
six year-old Collins agonised over Pat's letters inviting
him to America. He took long lonely walks through
London's dockland, seeing the ships leave for the
New World, wondering should he go himself. War
meant conscription would come, bringing with it an

unthinkable choice: to become a conscientious objector, a course repugnant to his warrior soul, or to don a British uniform and fight for the Crown.

Collins solved the problem in his own inimitable way. He put on an Irish uniform and went to fight for Ireland, in the 1916 Easter Rebellion in Dublin. He was captured and sent to Frongoch Internment Camp in Wales, the Republican University as it was known. It was here, in prison, that he began to think out a new philosophy of warfare and to re-organise the Irish Republican Brotherhood, the I.R.B., which later spearheaded the fight for Irish independence and led to the creation of modern Ireland. He was also the founder of modern urban guerilla warfare, the first freedom fighter, or urban terrorist. Mao Tse tSung studied his methods. And Yatzik Shamir, the former Prime Minister of Israel, was so impressed with Collins that not alone did he study him, he took the codename "Micail" for his Irgun unit during the Israeli war of independence against the British.

Before considering his career and writings, I must briefly diverge to look at Collins' origins and examine what led him to a London counting house in the first place. He was born, the youngest of eight children, on a ninety-acre farm, a good holding for Catholics of the time, near Clonakilty in West Cork in 1890, to a remarkable set of parents. His father was nearly forty years older than his mother, Marianne, and was in his seventy-sixth year when Michael arrived. Neither parent had much formal education but they both knew French, Latin, Greek, Irish and English. And, apart from being an expert farmer and veterinarian,

Michael senior was also noted for his knowledge of astronomy, mathematics, and for his skill as a builder. The Collins, or the O'Coileain as they were known in Irish, were once a very considerable Munster clan. And the family, both in Michael Collins' day and in our own, is recognised as being unusually intelligent and well-doing.

However Michael senior died when young Michael was six, leaving Marianne to run the farm and look after the eight children. One by one, all the children were forced to emigrate, until only Johnnie, who ran the farm after Marianne contracted cancer, and Michael, who was then fourteen, were left at home.

There was at the time a tradition of recruiting for the British postal service in the Clonakilty area. When a baby boy was born, the neighbours' first comment on looking into the pram was "musha 'tis the fine sorter he'll make". Collins attended a class in Clonakilty which prepared pupils for the post office exams, and, at the age of sixteen, crossed over to London to live with his sister Hannie and take up work as a boy clerk in Kensington Post Office Savings Bank.

Collins became very active in the Irish-Ireland life of London, joining the Gaelic League to learn Irish, and the Gaelic Athletic Association to play Gaelic football and hurling, one of the most skilful and dangerous stick games in the world. He was a natural athlete, a particularly fine hurler, with a cloud-burst temperament that meant he either initiated or was drawn to any fights that broke out on the field. His deep belief in these associations and commitment to Gaelic culture are clear in his essay "Freedom Within

Grasp, For Ourselves to Achieve It". He found time too to continue his studies and to become a regular theatre goer, a particular fan of George Bernard Shaw. He was an omnivorous reader, mopping up anything he could find in the way of Irish nationalist literature and a variety of other authors including Conrad, Arnold Bennet, Chesterton, Hardy, Meredith, Swinburne as well as Irish literary figures such as Wilde, Yeats, Pádraic Colum and James Stephens.

And now we come to the point where Collins' shadow begins to fall across contemporary Ireland. In or around 1914 he was sworn into the oath-bound secret society, the Irish Republican Brotherhood, by a fellow Corkman, Sam Maguire. The then political situation was that Ireland had lost its parliament under the Act of Union of 1800. Its culture, industry and population had suffered grievously as a result, the Great Famine is only one of the many ills on which we need not dwell here. But in 1914 Ireland seemed to be in a fair way of getting its own government back again. At Westminster the Irish Parliamentary Party, the constitutionalist wing of Irish nationalist self-assertion, had brought Home Rule to the Statute Book under the leadership of John Redmond. Ireland seemed to be on the verge of achieving its own parliament. But there was opposition.

In the north of the country, the Protestants of North-Eastern Ulster clung to their Scottish ancestry and British links. They wanted to remain in union with Westminster just exactly as do the unionists of today. More importantly, like today's unionists, they were backed to the point, and some would say beyond the point, of treason in this attitude by the British Conservative Party. The Tories dealt a death blow to Home Rule, which had been passed by a democratically elected majority in the House of Commons, by two major acts of defiance of Parliament. One was their sponsorship of the illegal gun running at Larne which put teeth into the Protestants' resolution to resist. The second was their even more efficacious sponsorship of a move within the British Army to refuse to proceed against their rebellious co-religionists, known as the Curragh mutiny.

The Conservatives were not acting out of affection for the Ulster Protestants. But they used the Orangemen, as they were known after the Orange society to which so many of them belonged, as a weapon in domestic British politics to undermine the Liberal Government led by Prime Minister Asquith which had been driven to sponsor Home Rule through dependence on Irish Party support for its majority. The tactic, known as playing the Orange Card, was invented by Randolph Churchill, Winston's father. He coined the phrase "Ulster will fight and Ulster will be right". As his grandson, also called Randolph, wrote sixty years later: "that pithy phrase explains why Ulster is part of the United Kingdom today".

The I.R.B., or Fenian movement, distrusted British politics and politicians as a matter of dogma. The Fenians did not accept that Britain would ever confer Home Rule, or any form of independence on Ireland unless it were forced to, not by parliamentary methods, but by physical force. For those with a taste for symbolism I may digress to remark that the constitutionalist John Redmond is now seldom heard of in Ireland. Today Ireland's premier sporting trophy is the Sam Maguire Cup which is played for each year in the All-Ireland Football Final at Croke Park. And Northern Ireland is still something of a political football.

However to revert to Michael Collins. In his everyday working life Collins sought to broaden his range of experience by moving from the Post Office to a firm of stockbrokers, Horne and Co, from there to a clerkship in the Board of Trade and finally, perhaps because of his brother Pat's urgings, he moved, to gain a flavour of American business life, to the Guaranty Trust Company of New York's London Office where war found him.

He found his own war in Dublin in Easter 1916. It was a rebellion that should not have been allowed to happen. Had Home Rule for all Ireland not been aborted by the strength of the unionist/conservative alliance, there would have been no subsequent Anglo-Irish war, no civil war, no Partition and no I.R.A., or Northern Ireland problem today. But that searing week of flame and folly during Easter 1916 claimed the lives of some of the people Collins most admired: Tom Clarke, James Connolly, Sean Hurley, Seán Mac-Diarmada, Joseph Plunkett. To him their deaths were a debt owed, a charge against freedom, which England would repay. However, he would not present his bill for retribution by means of conventional warfare.

He still believed in fighting. In the parliamentary game as played at Westminster the rules were so arranged that the outnumbered Irish nationalists always lost. Collins now understood also that static warfare, i.e. seizing a stronghold, be it a building such as Dublin's General Post Office in which he fought during the rebellion, or a mountain top, and then slugging it out with rifles and shot guns against an adversary who possessed heavy artillery, would continue to provide the Irish with heroes and martyrs— and the British with victories.

Instead Collins evolved a new concept of guerilla warfare based not on the capture of the enemy's bricks and mortar, but of its information. Traditionally, Dublin Castle, the seat of British administration in Ireland, had used a network of spies and informers to infiltrate and then snuff out movements directed at securing Irish independence. Collins perfected a system of spying on the spies. Every important branch of the Castle system, be it banking, policing, the railways, the postal service, was infiltrated by his agents. They were not highly trained, C.I.A.-style operatives, but ordinary men and women, people whom nobody had ever taken notice of before. Collins gave them a belief in themselves, a courage they did not know they possessed, and they in return gave him a complete picture of how their masters operated.

A secretary in Military Intelligence saw to it that Collins had a copy of the Colonel's orders to the Captain before the officer received the originals. A railway porter carried dispatches, the docker smuggled in revolvers, the detective told him who the informers were—and the Squad used the revolvers to deal with them. The Squad was his particular brainchild. For the first time in her history the Irish had a team of assassins trained to eliminate informers. I once handled the weapons used by the Squad, parabellums, '45s, Colt revolvers, and it was quite a chilling moment to be told: "Each of those revolvers killed at least six men". I later realised of course that, in the scale of modern warfare, the totals were tiny. Collins was careful about wasting human life. He struck selectively, to achieve the maximum political and psychological advantage. As he said himself, "England could always replace a detective. But the man can not step into the dead man's shoes—and his knowledge." He thus demoralised the hitherto invincible Royal Irish Constabulary, the armed police force which operated from fortified barracks and held Ireland for the Crown.

Action was not confined to Dublin. Generalised warfare broke out all over the country as the British introduced new men and new methods in a vain effort to counter the guerilla tactics of Collins' Active Service Units and the Flying Columns of Volunteers, which lived on the run, eating and sleeping where they could.

Held back from making a full scale use of their Army by the force of world opinion, largely Irish-American opinion, the British tried to fight a "police war" carried on by hastily formed forces of ex-service men and officers troubled by little discipline and less conscience. The Black and Tans and the Auxiliaries wrote new chapters of horror in the bloodstained story of the Anglo-Irish relationship. Reprisals for the activities of Collins and his colleagues included the burning of homes and creameries, random murder and the widespread use of torture. Through it all Collins lived a "life on the bicycle". The most wanted man in Europe, he smiled his way through a hundred hold-ups never wearing a disguise, never missing an appointment, never certain where he would spend the night.

One of his central ideas was derived from G.K. Chesterton's *The Man Who Was Thursday*. He was given the book by Joseph Plunkett, his immediate superior in 1916. Plunkett, who was dying of tuberculosis, took part in the fighting and was married in his cell, ten minutes before facing a firing squad. Obviously any relic of such a figure would be prized by his lieutenant. And Collins prized in particular the advice of the Chief Anarchist in the Chesterton book: "if you don't seem to be hiding nobody hunts you out". Accordingly, Collins never seemed to be hiding. He always wore good suits, neatly pressed. And time after time, this young businessman was passed through police cordons unsearched, with his pockets stuffed with incriminating documents. It seems to be an iron law with policemen both in Collins' time and ours, that terrorists are not expected to wear pin-striped suits and clean collars and ties.

He had a network of safe houses and secret rooms where he transacted business. One room I examined was reached by pulling a lever which caused the bottom half of a kitchen dresser to swing upwards on hinges. Collins used to work in the house, until it was raided and then slip into the secret room and work away until the soldiers surrounding the house moved out of the garden. None of them ever realised that there was an unaccounted for window in the back wall of the house.

In addition to his campaign of warfare Collins ran a national loan which was banned by the British so that its advertisement or sale became illegal. Yet the loan was fully subscribed and every subscriber got a receipt. He was President of the omnipresent I.R.B. which regarded him as the real President of the Irish Republic, and Minister for Finance in the *Sinn Féin* Cabinet. In addition, he was Director of Intelligence of the Irish Republican Army (I.R.A.). Any one of those jobs would have consumed the energy of an ordinary man, but Collins combined them all efficiently and effectively.

He combined a mind like a laser beam with a hawk-like eye for detail. Nothing escaped his attention. Everything attracted his interest. Shaw's latest play, the way the Swiss organised a Citizen Army, Benjamin Franklin's proposals for dealing with loyalists, or the latest edition of *Popular Mechanics*. An article in this journal in November of 1920 led to the first use in warfare of the Thomson gun. Collins saw the article on the recently invented weapon and had enquiries made about "this splendid thing"[1], which led to the Irish-American leader Joseph McGarrity of Philadelphia buying five hundred of the weapons. Two Irish-American ex-officers were sent to Ireland to train the I.R.A. in the use of the weapons. Only a handful got through the American customs, but these were duly used in a number of Dublin ambushes.

Collins was tough and abrasive with his male, and sometimes female, colleagues. But he was gentle and playful with children and old people. Throughout the eighteen months that Eamon de Valera was in America, on a propaganda and fund-raising mission, which lasted most of the Anglo-Irish war, Collins risked his life to call each week to his absent chief's family, bringing them money and companionship.

Eventually the war effort that Collins had spearheaded drove the British to a conference table and a settlement as foreseeable as it was unpalatable to many Irishmen and women, a partitioned Irish Free State that would owe allegiance to the Crown. It was a deal which had been foreshadowed to de Valera in four days of talks between himself and Lloyd George, the British Prime Minister, in London during July 1921. But de Valera did not want to be the man who faced up to the implications of that deal. Instead he repaid the kindness Collins had shown his family in Machiavellian fashion. He stayed away himself from the opprobrious negotiations but manipulated Collins into going to London as part of the delegation which signed the Anglo-Irish Treaty of December 6th, 1921, the constitutional foundation document of modern Ireland. Collins, who took the leading part in the Treaty's negotiation, faced one of the most powerful British delegations ever assembled. Winston Churchill only ranked fourth on the team which was led by Lloyd George and included the Lord Chancellor, Lord Birkenhead and the leader of the Conservative Party Austen Chamberlain. Subsequently Collins became Chairman of the Executive Council (in effect the Government) of the Irish Free State which emerged, and, later, Commander-in-Chief of the Army.

The Treaty did not yield the Republic he had hoped for but it provided what Collins prophetically termed a "stepping stone" to today's Irish Republic. All the other stepping stones to the tragedy of today's Northern Ireland situation were part of that negotiation too. In a very real sense Collins' premature death was caused by the forces which still rage about the North-Eastern corner of the land and people he fought for. The story of his life explains present day news from Belfast. He was forced into an impossible, janus-faced policy. On the one hand, as head of the infant Provisional Government of Southern Ireland, he argued fiercely for the Treaty's potential for democracy and freedom as we can read in many of his articles and speeches. He engaged in civil war to defend it against de Valera and his former comrades in the I.R.A.

On the other hand, the plight of the Catholics in Northern Ireland, subject to pogrom and prejudice, drove him to arm secretly the I.R.A. in the North. He did everything in his power to destabilise the northern state. He organised burnings, raids, kidnappings; and once, when some of his followers faced execution, he sent two former members of the Squad over to England to shoot the British executioners who were detailed to hang them. At the last moment the I.R.A. men were reprieved. So were the hangmen.

One of the great questions of Irish history is: If Collins had lived longer would he have brought fire or prosperity to his country? Or would he have died of drink or disillusionment at the effects of the civil war which broke out over the terms of the Treaty? Certainly he had more business acumen and vision than any of his contemporaries. He foresaw a role for Ireland in Europe long before the E.U. was ever heard of. He preaches in one essay that Ireland should study the lessons of German scientific advancement, Danish agriculture, and bring them back home to develop a distinctive Irish economy and culture of its own. He loved the Irish language, but not merely as a medium of expression. As we learn in "Distinctive Culture, Ancient Irish Civilization" he saw in the language a method of thinking and ultimately of acting, more suited to Ireland than the Anglo-Saxon inheritance. He believed in personal initiative, writing in "Building Up Ireland, Resources To Be Developed"

> Millionaires can spend their surplus wealth bestowing libraries broadcast upon the world. But who will say that the benefits accruing could be compared with those arising from a condition of things in which the people themselves everywhere, in the city, town, and village were prosperous enough to buy their own books and to put together their own local libraries in which they could take a personal interest and acquire knowledge in proportion to that interest.

Tragically we will never know how this marvellous man might have developed. For as the German poet Heine once remarked, the Irish always pull down a noble stag. Our Irish Siegfried kept his appointment in Samarra a couple of months short of his thirty-second birthday in a remote Cork valley known in Irish as Beál na mBláth, the Mouth of Flowers. He died during the Civil War not far from where he was born, in an ambush laid by a former comrade in arms, a man who during the Anglo-Irish War had undergone sadistic tortures at the hands of British Intelligence Officers rather than betray his boyhood friend, Michael Collins.

Collins' career is a paradigm of the tragedy of modern Ireland, the suffering, the waste of talent, the hope, the bedevilling effects of history and nomenclature whereby one man's terrorist is another man's freedom fighter. Like Prometheus, Collins stole fire. Like Prometheus he paid for his feat and much of what he set about doing remains undone. But his name burns brightly wherever the Irish meet. Michael Collins was the man who made modern Ireland possible.

Tim Pat Coogan

---

1 Described by Sean Cronin, The McGarrity Papers, Anvil Books, Tralee, Co. Kerry, 1978, p. 98.

Publisher's Note to the Original Edition

The following Notes drafted by General Collins early in August and apparently intended for public utterance, probably to *An Dáil*, were without correction by him. Obviously no one can now say what the changing circumstances might have caused him to alter or add.

The Notes are now printed as an introduction to the articles written by General Collins.

NOTES BY GENERAL MICHAEL COLLINS

August, 1922

After a national struggle sustained through many centuries, we have today in Ireland a native Government deriving its authority solely from the Irish people, and acknowledged by England and the other nations of the world.

Through those centuries—through hopes and through disappointments—the Irish people have struggled to get rid of a foreign Power which was preventing them from exercising their simple right to live and to govern themselves as they pleased—which tried to destroy our nationality, our institutions, which tried to abolish our customs and blot out our civilization,—all that made us Irish, all that united us as a nation.

But Irish nationality survived. It did not perish when native government was destroyed, and a foreign military despotism was set up. And for this reason, that it was not made by the old native government and it could not be destroyed by the foreign usurping government. It was the national spirit which created the old native government, and not the native government which created the national spirit. And nothing that the foreign government could do could destroy the national spirit.

But though it survived, the soul of the nation drooped and weakened. Without the protection of a native government we were exposed to the poison of foreign ways. The national character was infected and the life of the nation was endangered. We had armed risings and political agitation. We were not strong enough to put out the foreign Power until the national consciousness was fully re-awakened. This was why the Gaelic Movement and *Sinn Féin* were necessary for our last successful effort. Success came with the inspiration which the new national movement gave to our military and political effort. The Gaelic spirit working through the *Dáil* and the Army was irresistible.

In this light we must look at the present situation.

The new spirit of self-reliance and our splendid unity, and an international situation which we were able to use to our advantage, enabled our generation to make the greatest and most successful national effort in our history.

The right of Ireland as a nation under arms to decide its own destiny was acknowledged. We were invited to a Peace Conference. With the authority of Ireland's elected representatives negotiations were entered into between the two belligerent nations in order to find a basis of peace.

During the war we had gathered strength by the justice of our cause, and by the way in which we had carried on the struggle. We had organised our own government, and had made the most of our military resources. The united nation showed not only endurance and courage but a humanity which was in marked contrast with the conduct of the enemy. All this gave us a moral strength in the negotiations of which we took full advantage.

But in any sane view our military resources were terribly slender in the face of those of the British Empire which had just emerged victorious from the world war. It was obvious what would have been involved in a renewal of armed conflict on a scale which we had never met before. And it was obvious what we should have lost in strength if the support of the world which had hitherto been on our side had been alienated, if Ireland had rejected terms which most nations would have regarded as terms we could honourably accept.

We had not an easy task.

We were faced with a critical military situation over against an enemy of infinitely greater potential strength. We had to face the pride and prejudice of a powerful nation which had claimed for centuries to hold Ireland as a province. We had to face all the traditions, and political experience, and strength of the British nation. And on our flank we had a section of our own people who had identified their outlook and interests with those of Britain.

It may be claimed that we did not fail in our task. We got the substance of freedom, as has already been made real before our eyes by the withdrawal of the British power.

And the people approved. And they were anxious to use the freedom secured. *The national instinct was sound*—that the essence of our struggle was *to secure freedom to order our own life*, without attaching undue importance to the formulas under which that freedom would be expressed. The people knew that our government could and would be moulded by the nation itself according to its needs. The nation would make the government, not the government the nation.

But on the return of Ireland's representatives from London, Mr. de Valera, who was then leader of the nation, condemned the Treaty in a public statement, while supporting similar proposals for peace which he described as differing "only by a shadow".

But he, and all the Deputies, joined in discussing and voting on the Treaty, and after full discussion and expressions of opinion from all parts of the country, the Treaty was approved.

And Mr. de Valera declared that there was a constitutional way of solving our differences. He expressed his readiness to accept the decision of the people. He resigned office, and a Provisional Government was formed to act with *Dáil Éireann*.

Two duties faced that Government:

(1) To take over the Executive from the English, and to maintain public order during the transition from foreign to native government;

and

(2) To give shape in a constitution to the freedom secured.

If the Government had been allowed to carry out these duties no difficulty would have arisen with

England, who carried out her part by evacuating her army and her administration. No trouble would have arisen among our own people. And the general trend of development, and the undoubted advantages of unity, would have brought the North-East quietly into union with the rest of the country, as soon as a stable national government had been established into which they could have come with confidence.

Mr. de Valera, and those who supported him in the *Dáil*, were asked to take part in the interim government, without prejudice to their principles, and their right to oppose the ratification of the Treaty at the elections.

They were asked to help in keeping an orderly united nation with the greatest possible strength over against England, exercising the greatest possible peaceful pressure towards the union of all Ireland, and with the greatest amount of credit for us in the eyes of the world, and with the greatest advantage to the nation itself in having a strong united government to start the departments of State, and to deal with the urgent problems of housing, land, hunger, and unemployment.

They did not find it possible to accept this offer of patriotic service.

Another offer was then made.

If they would not join in the work of transition, would they not co-operate in preserving order to allow that transition peacefully to take place? Would they not co-operate in keeping the army united, free from political bias, so as to preserve its strength for the proper purpose of defending the country in the exercise of its rights?

This also was refused.

It must be remembered that the country was emerging from a revolutionary struggle. And, as was to be expected, some of our people were in a state of excitement, and it was obviously the duty of all leaders to direct the thoughts of the people away from violence and into the steady channels of peace and obedience to authority. No one could have been blind to the course things were bound to take if this duty were neglected.

It was neglected, and events took their course.

Our ideal of nationality was distorted in hair-splitting over the meaning of "sovereignty" and other foreign words, under advice from minds dominated by English ideas of nationality; and, led away, some soon got out of control and betook themselves to the very methods we had learned to detest in the English and had united to drive out of the country.

By the time the *Árd Fheis* met the drift had become apparent. And the feeling in favour of keeping the national forces united was so strong that a belated agreement was arrived at. In return for a postponement of the elections, the Anti-Treaty Party pledged themselves to allow the work of the Provisional Government to proceed.

What came of that pledge?

Attempts to stampede meetings by revolver shootings, to wreck trains, the suppression of free speech, of the liberty of the Press, terrorisation and sabotage of a kind that we were familiar with a year ago. And with what object? With the sole object of preventing the people from expressing their will, and of making the government of Ireland by the representatives of the people as impossible as the English Government was made impossible by the united forces a year ago.

The policy of the Anti-Treaty Party had now become clear—to prevent the people's will from being carried out because it differed from their own, to create trouble in order to break up the only possible national government, and to destroy the Treaty with utter recklessness as to the consequences.

A section of the army, in an attempt at a military despotism, seized public buildings, took possession of the Chief Courts of Law of the Nation, dislocating private and national business, reinforced the Belfast Boycott which had been discontinued by the people's government, and "commandeered" public and private funds, and the property of the people.

Met by this reckless and wrecking opposition, and yet unwilling to use force against our own countrymen, we made attempt after attempt at conciliation.

We appealed to the soldiers to avoid strife, to let the old feelings of brotherhood and solidarity continue.

We met and made advances over and over again to the politicians, standing out alone on the one fundamental point on which we owed an unquestioned duty to the people—that we must maintain for them the position of freedom they had secured. We could get no guarantee that we would be allowed to carry out that duty.

The country was face to face with disaster, economic ruin, and the imminent danger of the loss of the position we had won by the national effort. If order could not be maintained, if no National Government was to be allowed to function, a vacuum would be created, into which the English would be necessarily drawn back. To allow that to happen would have been the greatest betrayal of the Irish people, whose one wish was to take and to secure and to make use of the freedom which had been won.

Seeing the trend of events, soldiers from both sides met to try and reach an understanding, on the basis that the people were admittedly in favour of the Treaty, that the only legitimate government could be one based on the people's will and that the practicable course was to keep the peace, and to make use of the position we had secured.

Those honourable efforts were defeated by the politicians. But at the eleventh hour an agreement was reached between Mr. de Valera and myself for which I have been severely criticised.

It was said that I gave away too much, that I went too far to meet them, that I had exceeded my powers in making a pact which, to some extent, interfered with the people's right to make a free and full choice at the elections.

It was a last effort on our part to avoid strife, to prevent the use of force by Irishmen against Irishmen. We refrained from opposing the Anti-Treaty Party at the elections. We stood aside from political conflict, so that, so far as we were concerned, our opponents might retain the full number of seats which they had held in the previous *Dáil*. And I undertook, with the approval of the Government, that they should hold four out of the nine offices in the new Ministry. They calculated that in this way they would have the same position in the new *Dáil* as in the old. But their calculations were upset by the people themselves, and they then dropped all pretence of representing the people, and turned definitely against them.

The Irregular Forces in the Four Courts continued in their mutinous attitude. They openly defied the newly expressed will of the people. On the pretext of enforcing a boycott of Belfast goods, they raided and looted a Dublin garage, and when the leader of the raid was arrested by the National Forces, they retaliated by the seizure of one of the principal officers of the National Army.

Such a challenge left two courses open to the National Government: either to betray its trust and surrender to the mutineers, or to fulfil its duty and carry out the work entrusted to it by the people.

The Government did its duty. Having given them one last opportunity to accept the situation, to obey the people's will, when the offer was rejected the Government took the necessary measures to protect the rights and property of the people and to disperse the armed bands which had outlawed themselves and were preying upon the nation.

Unbelievers had said that there was not, and had never been, an Irish Nation capable of harmonious, orderly development. That it was not the foreign invader but the character of the Irish themselves which throughout history had made of our country a scene of strife.

We knew this to be a libel. Our historians had shown our nationality as existing from legendary ages, and through centuries of foreign oppression.

What made Ireland a nation was a common way of life, which no military force, no political change could destroy. Our strength lay in a common ideal of how a people should live, bound together by mutual ties, and by a devotion to Ireland which shrank from no individual sacrifice. This consciousness of unity carried us to success in our last great struggle.

In that spirit we fought and won. The old fighting spirit was as strong as ever, but it had gained a fresh strength in discipline in our generation. Every county sent its boys whose unrecorded deeds were done in the spirit of Cuchulain at the Ford.

But the fight was not for one section of the nation against another, but for Ireland against the foreign oppressor. We fought for that for which alone fighting is really justified—for national freedom, for the right of the whole people to live as a nation.

And we fought in a way we had never fought before, and Ireland won a victory she had never won before.

The foreign Power was withdrawn. The civil administration passed into the hands of the elected representatives of the people. The fight with the English enemy was ended. The function of our armed forces was changed. Their duty now was to preserve the freedom won—to enable the people to use it, to realise that for which they had fought—a free, prosperous, self-governing Gaelic Ireland.

Differences as to political ideals such as remained or might develop amongst us—these were not a matter for the army, these were not a matter for force, for violence.

Under the democratic system which was being established by the representatives of the people—the freest and most democratic system yet devised—the rights of every minority were secured, and the fullest opportunity was open for every section of opinion to express and advocate its views by appeal to reason and patriotic sentiment.

In these circumstances, the only way in which individual views could be rightly put forward by patriotic Irishmen was by peaceful argument and appeal. The time had come when the best policy for Ireland could be promoted in ways which would keep the nation united—strong against the outside world, and settling its own differences peacefully at home.

To allow such a situation to develop successfully required only common sense and patriotism in the political leaders. No one denied that the new Government had the support of the people.

Of all forms of government a democracy allows the greatest freedom—the greatest possibilities for the good of all. But such a government, like all governments, must be recognised and obeyed.

The first duty of the new Government was to maintain public order, security of life, personal liberty, and property.

The duty of the leaders was to secure free discussion of public policy, and to get all parties to recognise that, while they differed, they were fellow-citizens of one free State. It should have been the political glory of Ireland to show that our differences of opinion could express themselves so as to promote, and not to destroy, the national life.

The army had to recognise that they were the servants and not the masters of the people—that their function was not to impose their will on the people but to secure to the people the right to express their own will and to order their lives accordingly.

All this might indeed appear obvious to all patriotic persons.

But with the removal of the pressure of the English enemy, the spirit of order, and unity, and devotion to Ireland as a whole was suddenly weakened in some directions. The readiness to fight remained after the occasion for fighting was gone. Some lost grasp of the ideal for which they had fought and magnified personal differences into a conflict of principles.

The road was clear for us to march forward, peaceful and united, to achieve our goal and the revival of our Gaelic civilization. The peace and order necessary for that progress was rudely broken. The united forward movement was held up by an outbreak of anarchic violence.

The nation which had kept the old heroic temper, but had learnt to govern it so that violence should be directed against the national enemy, and its differences should be matters of friendly rivalry, found itself faced with a small minority determined to break up the national unity and to destroy the government in which the nation had just shown its confidence.

They claimed to be fighting for the nation. That might be possible if there were any enemies of the nation opposing them. There are not. Resolved to fight, they are fighting, not against an enemy, but against their own nation. Blind to facts, and false to ideals, they are making war on the Irish people.

To conceal this truth they claim to be opposing the National Government which they declare to be a usurpation. In view of the elections this is absurd enough. No one can deny that the present Government rests on the will of the people, the sole authority for any government. And what was the usurpation they complained of? Simply that the Government refused to allow authority to be wrested from it by an armed minority. If it is not right for a National Government to keep public order, to prevent murder, arson, and brigandage, what are the duties of a government?

But it is not the fact that they have directed their fight against the National Government and the National Army. It was against the Irish people themselves that they directed their operations.

The anti-national character of their campaign became clear when we saw them pursuing exactly the same course as the English Black and Tans. They robbed and destroyed, not merely for the sake of loot, and from a criminal instinct to destroy (though in any candid view of their operations these elements must be seen to have been present) but on a plan, and for a definite purpose. Just as the English claimed that they were directing their attack against a "murder gang", so the irregulars claim that they are making war on a "usurping" government.

But, in reality, the operations and the motives in both cases were, and are, something quite different— namely, the persecution and terrorism of the unarmed population, and the attempt by economic destruction, famine, and violence, to "make an appropriate hell" in Ireland, in the hope of breaking up the organised National Government and undermining the loyalty of the people.

And of what is it all the inevitable outcome? Of the course to which the unthinking enthusiasm of some was directed when they were told repeatedly that it might be necessary to turn their arms against their brothers and to wade through Irish blood.

But the true nature of the whole movement has now demonstrated itself so that no one can doubt it. A tree is known by its fruits—we have seen the fruits. The Irish people will be confirmed in its conviction that those fruits are deadly. They will have no sympathy with anarchy and violence.

The Irish people know that true Irish nationality does not express itself in these ways. They know it is the Government, and not those who call themselves Republicans, who are upholding the national ideal.

The tactics of disruption and disorder were antinational in paralysing the energies which were needed for building up the new Ireland.

Worse still, their violence and the passions it aroused have broken up the united concentration on the revival of our language and of our Irish life.

Worst of all, their action has been a crime against the nation in this—that the anarchy and ruin they were bringing about was undermining the confidence of the nation in itself. So far as it succeeded it was proving that our enemies were right, that we were incapable of self-government. When left to ourselves in freedom we could show nothing of the native civilization we had claimed as our own.

The Black and Tans with all their foreign brutality were unable to make of Ireland "an appropriate hell". The irregulars brought their country to the brink of a real hell, the black pit in which our country's name and credit would have sunk, in which our existence as a distinct nation, *our belief in ourselves as a nation* might have perished for ever. If they had succeeded in destroying the National Government, and reducing the country to anarchy, the greatest evil would have been, not that the English would have come back, that would indeed have been terrible enough, *but that they would have been welcomed back, that they would have come not as enemies, but as the only protectors who could bring order and peace.*

For hundreds of years we had preserved our national hopes. We were on the point of achieving them, but when the real test came the national consciousness lapsed in the minds of some whom the nation had trusted. The wrong done was not merely to the material prospects of the nation *but to its soul.*

The calamity was unnecessary. There lies the wrong to the nation. A simple acceptance of the people's will! That was all that was asked of them. What principle could such an acceptance have violated?

All further measures necessary will be taken to maintain peace and order.

We have to face realities.

There is no British Government any longer in Ireland. It is gone. It is no longer the enemy. We have now a native government, constitutionally elected, and it is the duty of every Irish man and woman to obey it. Anyone who fails to obey it is an enemy of the people and must expect to be treated as such.

We have to learn that attitudes and actions which were justifiable when directed against an alien administration, holding its position by force, are wholly unjustifiable against a native government which exists only to carry out the people's will, and which can be changed the moment it ceases to do so. We have to learn that freedom imposes responsibilities.

This parliament is now the controlling body. With the unification of the administration it will be clothed with full authority. Through the parliament the people have the right, and the power, to get the constitution, the legislation, and the economic and educational arrangements they desire. The courts of law, which are now our own courts, will be reorganised to make them national in character, and the people will be able to go to them with confidence of receiving justice.

That being so, the Government believes it will have the whole force of public opinion behind it in dealing sternly with all unlawful acts of every kind, no matter under what name of political or patriotic, or any other policy that may be carried out.

The National Army, and the new Irish Police Force, acting in obedience to the Administration, will defend the freedom and rights of the Nation, and will put down crime of whatever nature, sectarian, agrarian or confiscatory.

In the special circumstances I have had to stress the Government's determination to establish the foundations of the state, to preserve the very life of the Nation. But a policy of development is engaging the attention of all departments, and will shortly be made known.

We have a difficult task before us. We have taken over an alien and cumbersome administration. We have to begin the upbuilding of the nation with foreign tools. But before we can scrap them we must first forge fresh Gaelic ones to take their place, and must temper their steel.

But if we will all work together in a mutually helpful spirit, recognising that we all seek the same end, the good of Ireland, the difficulties will disappear.

The Irish Nation is the whole people, of every class, creed, and outlook. We recognise no distinction. It will be our aim to weld all our people nationally together who have hitherto been divided in political and social and economic outlook.

Labour will be free to take its rightful place as an element in the life of the nation. In Ireland more than in any other country lies the hope of the rational adjustment of the rights and interests of all sections, and the new government starts with the resolve that Irish Labour shall be free to play the part which belongs to it in helping to shape our industrial and commercial future.

The freedom, strength, and greatness of the nation will be measured by the independence, economic well-being, physical strength and intellectual greatness of the people.

A new page of Irish history is beginning.

We have a rich and fertile country—a sturdy and intelligent people. With peace, security and union, no one can foresee the limits of greatness and well-being to which our country may not aspire.

But it is not only within our country that we have a new outlook. Ireland has now a recognised international status. Not only as an equal nation in association with the British nations, but as a member of the wider group forming the League of Nations. As a member of these groups, Ireland's representatives will have a voice in international affairs, and will use that voice to promote harmony and peaceful intercourse among all friendly nations.

In this way Ireland will be able to play a part in the new world movement, and to play that part in accordance with the old Irish tradition of an independent distinctive Irish nation, at harmony, and in close trading, cultural, and social relations, with all other friendly nations.

In this sense our outlook is new. But our national aim remains the same—a free, united Irish nation and united Irish race all over the world, bent on achieving the common aim of Ireland's prosperity and good name.

Underlying the change of outlook there is this continuity of outlook.

For 700 years the united effort has been to get the English out of Ireland. For this end, peaceful internal development had to be left neglected, and the various interests which would have had distinct aims had to sink all diversity and unite in the effort of resistance, and the ejection of the English power.

This particular united effort is now at an end. But it is to be followed by a new united effort for the actual achievement of the common goal. The negative work of expelling the English power is done. The positive work of building a Gaelic Ireland in the vacuum left has now to be undertaken.

This requires not merely unity, but diversity in unity. Each Irish interest, each phase of Irish life, industrial, commercial, cultural, social, must find expression and have a voice in the development of the country, partly by the government, and partly by co-operation and individual effort.

But they must express themselves and use their influence, not in hostility to one another, but in co-operation. And in furthering their special aims, they must do so in the light of the common ideal—a united, distinctive Irish nationality.

And there must be, to reach this ideal, and particularly so at this moment, allegiance to and support of the National Government, democratically elected. At least to the extent of assisting it to restore and maintain peace and public order, rights of life and property according to law, freedom for all individuals, parties, and creeds, to express themselves lawfully.

This is why we claim that the measures to restore order which we have taken are not repressive. They are seen to be carrying the liberative movement to completion, clearing away the *débris* in order to lay firm and solid the foundations on which to build the new Ireland.

Those who are restoring order, not those who tried to destroy it, are the preservers of Irish nationality. Fidelity to the real Ireland lies in uniting to build up a real Ireland in conformity with our ideal, and not in disruption and destruction as a sacrifice to the false gods of foreign-made political formulas.

The ideal is no good unless it lights our present path. Otherwise it is but a vain sentiment, or misleading will-o'-the-wisp. We can all be faithful to what is our national ideal—the Ireland of poetic tradition, and the future Ireland which will one day be—the best of what our country was, and can be again, and the perfect freedom in which it alone can be the best.

It is because this ideal is not a fact now, that we must be faithful to it, and our faithfulness to it consists in making it a fact so far as we can in ourselves and in our day.

Accepting the freedom which we have here and now is to recognise facts and is to be faithful to the national ideal as taking the best practical means to achieve as much as we can of the ideal at the moment. We grasp the substance of freedom, and are true to Ireland in using that freedom to make an actual Ireland as near to the ideal one as possible. We have not got, and cannot get now at the moment, (certainly cannot get without sacrificing the hope of things more important and essential for our true ideal)—the political Republic. If we had got it, we should not necessarily be much further forward towards our true goal—a Gaelic Ireland.

We must be true to facts if we would achieve anything in this life. We must be true to our ideal, if we would achieve anything worthy. The Ireland to which we are true, to which we are devoted and faithful, is the ideal Ireland, which means there is always something more to strive for. The true devotion lies not in melodramatic defiance or self-sacrifice for something falsely said to exist, or for mere words and formalities, which are empty, and which might be but the house newly swept and garnished to which seven worse devils entered in. It is the steady, earnest effort in face of actual possibilities towards the solid achievement of our hopes and visions, the laying of stone upon stone of a building which is actual and in accordance with the ideal pattern.

In this way, what we can do in our time, being done in faithfulness to the traditions of the past, and to the vision of the future, becomes significant and glorified beyond what it is if looked at as only the day's momentary partial work.

This is where our Irish temperament, tenacity of the past, its vivid sense of past and future greatness, readiness for personal sacrifice, belief and pride in our race, can play an unique part, if it can stand out in its intellectual and moral strength, and shake off the weaknesses which long generations of subjection and inaction have imposed upon it.

Let the nation show its true and best character: use its courage, tenacity, clear swift intellect, its pride in the service of the national ideal as our reason directs us.

"ADVANCE AND USE OUR LIBERTIES"

In my opinion the Truce of July, 1921, could have been secured in December, 1920, at the time His Grace Archbishop Clune endeavoured to mediate, but the opportunity was lost through the too precipitate action of certain of our public men and public bodies.

The actions taken indicated an over-keen desire for peace, and although terms of Truce were virtually agreed upon, they were abandoned because the British leaders thought those actions indicated weakness, and they consequently decided to insist upon surrender of our arms. The result was the continuance of the struggle. British aggression went on unabated and our defence was kept up to the best of our ability.

I am not aware of any negotiations that preceded the Truce of July. I do know there was much visiting by well-meaning, but unauthorised persons. So far, however, as my knowledge goes, these did not have any effect on the communication from Mr. Lloyd George to President de Valera which opened up the period of correspondence between the two Governments and the subsequent negotiations in London. If there were any official conversations prior to the Lloyd George Letter, they took place entirely without my knowledge.

It has been variously stated that the Treaty was signed under duress.

I did not sign the Treaty under duress, except in the sense that the position as between Ireland and England, historically, and because of superior forces on the part of England, has always been one of duress.

The element of duress was present when we agreed to the Truce, because our simple right would have been to beat the English out of Ireland. There was an element of duress in going to London to negotiate. But there was not, and could not have been, any personal duress.

The threat of "immediate and terrible war" did not matter overmuch to me. The position appeared to be then exactly as it appears now. The British would not, I think, have declared terrible and immediate war upon us.

They had three courses of action open to them. First, to dissolve the parliaments and put their proposals before the country; second, to resume the war by courting openly and covertly breakages of the Truce (these breakages of the Truce might easily have come from either side); thirdly, to blockade Ireland, and at the same time encourage spasmodic internal conflict.

The first course of action seemed to me to be the most likely, and, as a result of a political win on our side either No. 2 or No. 3 would have been very easily managed by the British. A political reverse would have been more damaging to us than either 2 or 3. The threat of immediate and terrible war was probably bluff. The immediate tactics would surely have been to put the offer of July 20, which the British considered a very good offer, before the country, and, if rejected, they would have very little difficulty in carrying their own people into a war against Ireland.

Another thing I believe is that on resumption of hostilities the British would have been anxious to fight with us on the basis of belligerent rights. In such circumstances, I doubt if we would have been able to carry on a conflict with the success which had previously attended our efforts. I scarcely think that our resources would have been equal to bearing belligerent rights and responsibilities.

I am not impressed by the talk of duress, nor by threats of a declaration of immediate and terrible war. Britain has not made a declaration of war upon Egypt, neither has she made a declaration of war upon India. But is the conflict less terrible because of the absence of such declaration?

We must not be misled by words and phrases. Unquestionably the alternative to the Treaty, sooner or later, was war, and if the Irish Nation had accepted that, I should have gladly accepted it. The opponents of the Treaty have declared over and over again that the alternative to the Treaty was not war.

In my judgement, this was misleading the Irish Nation. The decision of the Irish Nation should not be given on a false basis. That was, and is, my own attitude, and if indeed, it be true, as the antagonists of the Treaty say, that the alternative to the Treaty was not war, where, then, is the heroism? Where, then, is the necessity for the future sacrifices that have been talked of so freely?

To me it would have been a criminal act to refuse to allow the Irish Nation to give its opinion as to whether it would accept this settlement or resume hostilities. That, I maintain, is a democratic stand. It has always been the stand of public representatives who are alive to their responsibilities.

The Irish struggle has always been for freedom— freedom from English occupation, from English interference, from English domination—not for freedom with any particular label attached to it.

What we fought for at any particular time was the greatest measure of freedom obtainable at that time, and it depended upon our strength whether the claim was greater than at another time or lesser than at another time.

When the national situation was very bad we lay inert; when it improved a little we looked for Repeal of the Union; when it receded again we looked for Home Rule under varying trade names; when it went still worse we spoke of some form of devolution. When our strength became greater our aim became higher, and we strove for a greater measure of freedom under the name of a Republic. But it was freedom we sought for, not the name of the form of government we should adopt when we got our freedom.

When I supported the approval of the Treaty at the meeting of *Dáil Éireann* I said it gave us freedom—

not the ultimate freedom which all nations hope for and struggle for, but freedom to achieve that end. And I was, and am now, fully alive to the implications of that statement.

Under the Treaty Ireland is about to become a fully constituted nation. The whole of Ireland, as one nation, is to compose the Irish Free State, whose parliament will have power to make laws for the peace, order, and good government of Ireland, with an executive responsible to that parliament.

This is the whole basis of the Treaty. It is the bedrock from which our status springs, and any later Act of the British Parliament derives its force from the Treaty only. We have got the present position by virtue of the Treaty, and any forthcoming Act of the British Legislature will, likewise, be by virtue of the Treaty.

It is not the definition of any status which would secure to us that status, but our power to make secure, and to increase what we have gained; yet, obtaining by the Treaty the constitutional status of Canada, and that status being one of freedom and equality, we are free to take advantage of that status, and we shall set up our Constitution on independent Irish lines. And no conditions mentioned afterwards in the Treaty can affect or detract from the powers which the mention of that status in the Treaty gives us, especially when it has been proved, has been made good, by the withdrawal out of Ireland of English authority of every kind.

In fact England has renounced all right to govern Ireland, and the withdrawal of her forces is the proof of this. With the evacuation secured by the Treaty has come the end of British rule in Ireland. No foreigner will be able to intervene between our Government and our people. Not a single British soldier, nor a single British official, will ever step again upon our shores, except as guests of a free people.

Our Government will have complete control of our army, our schools, and our trade. Our soldiers, our judges, our ministers will be the soldiers, judges, and ministers of the Irish Free State. We can send our own ambassadors to Washington, to Paris, to the Vatican; we can have our own representatives on the League of Nations (if we wish).

It was freedom we fought for—freedom from British interference and domination. Let us ask ourselves these few questions: Are the English going? To what extent are they going? If the Treaty is put into operation will they, for all practical purposes, be gone?

The answer to the first question is to be seen in the evacuation that is proceeding apace. We claimed that the Treaty would secure this evacuation. The claim is being fulfilled. The Auxiliaries are practically gone. The regular British military forces are rapidly following them. The answer to the second and third questions is that they remain for negligible purposes in that the extent to which they remain is negligible.

We shall have complete freedom for all our purposes. We shall be rid completely of British interference and British rule. We can establish in its place our own rule, and exactly what kind of rule we like. We can restore our Gaelic life in exactly what form we like. We can keep what we have gained and make it secure and strong. The little we have not yet gained we can go ahead and gain.

All other questions are really questions of arrangement, in which our voice shall be the deciding voice. Any names, any formulas, any figureheads, representing England's wish to conceal the extent of her departure, to keep some pretence of her power over us, which is now gone, will be but names, formulas, figureheads. England exercised her power over us simply by the presence of her forces—military forces, police forces, legal, and social forces.

Is it seriously to be suggested that in the new order, some functionary, no matter what we may call him, will serve the purpose of all these forces, or, apart from him, the particular interpretation of the words of a document?

The British Government could only be maintained by the presence of British forces. Once these are gone the British Government can no longer arrange the form our National Government and our National life will take, nor can they set any limits to either. If we wish to make our nation a free and a great and a good nation we can do so now. But we cannot do it if we are to fight among ourselves as to whether it is to be called *Saorstát* or *Poblacht*.

Whatever the name or the political phraseology, we cannot restore Ireland without a great united effort.

Any difficulty now in making a noble Irish-Ireland will lie in our people themselves and in the hundreds of years of anglicisation to which we have been subjected. The task before us, having got rid of the British, is to get rid of the British influences—to de-anglicise ourselves; for there are many among us who still cling to English ways, and any thought-lessness, any carelessness, will tend to keep things on the old lines—the inevitable danger of the proximity of the two nations.

Can any restriction or limitation in the Treaty prevent us making our nation great and potent? Can the presence of a representative of the British Crown, depending on us for his resources, prevent us from doing that? Can the words of a document as to what our status is prevent us from doing that? One thing only can prevent us—disunion among ourselves.

Can we not concentrate and unite, not on the negative, but on the positive, task of making a real Ireland distinct from Britain—a nation of our own?

The only way to get rid of British contamination and the evils of corrupt materialism is to secure a united Ireland intent on democratic ways, to make our free Ireland a fact, and not to keep it for ever in dreamland as something that will never come true, and which has no practical effect or reality except as giving rise to everlasting fighting and destruction, which seem almost to have become ends in themselves in the mind of some—some who appear to be unheeding and unmindful of what the real end is.

Ireland is one—perhaps the only—country in Europe which has now living hopes for a better civilization. We have a great opportunity. Much is within our grasp. Who can lay a finger on our liberties?

If any power menaces our liberties, we are in a stronger position than before to repel the aggressor. That position will grow stronger with each year of freedom if we will all unite for the aims we have in common.

Let us advance and use these liberties to make Ireland a shining light in a dark world, to reconstruct our ancient civilization on modern lines, to avoid the errors, the miseries, the dangers, into which other nations, with their false civilizations, have fallen.

In taking the Treaty we are not going in for the flesh-pots of the British Empire—not unless we wish to. It is futile to suppose that all these tendencies would disappear under freedom by some other name, or that the government of an externally associated nation, or of a Republic, any more than a Free State, would be able to suppress them, and to force Gaelicism upon the nation.

Whatever form of free government we had, it would be the Government of the Irish Nation. All the other elements, old Unionists, Home Rulers, Devolutionists, would have to be allowed freedom and self-expression. The only way to build the nation solid and Irish is to effect these elements in a friendly national way—by attraction, not by compulsion, making them feel themselves welcomed into the Irish Nation, in which they can join and become absorbed, as long ago the Geraldines and the de Burgos became absorbed.

The Treaty is already vindicating itself. The English Die-hards said to Mr. Lloyd George and his Cabinet: "You have surrendered." Our own Die-hards said to us: "You have surrendered." There is a simple test. Those who are left in possession of the battlefield have won.

ALTERNATIVE TO THE TREATY

Ireland "A Mother Country"

Document No. 2 Analysed

The main difference between the Treaty and the alternative proposals put forward by Mr. de Valera (known as Document No. 2) is that one is signed by the Plenipotentiaries of both nations and has been approved by the representatives of both nations; the other is not signed.

In my belief it would not be signed in its present form; not, indeed, that it contains much that is not in the Treaty, nor that it contains much that England objects to, but simply that in its construction it is too loose. Undoubtedly, in the application of its details we should constantly have been faced with conflicting interpretations leading to inevitable discordance.

It was claimed for the document by its sponsors that it would be approved by the English people; that, on the other hand, England never kept a Treaty, nor would she keep the present Treaty. The inference, of course, is that England would keep a Treaty which she had not signed but would not keep a Treaty which she had signed.

THE PATH TO FREEDOM

The document was not drafted by Mr. de Valera.
There is little difficulty in guessing the author. Domin-
ionism tinges every line. No Irishman who under-
stands the tradition and the history of Ireland would
think or write of his country's aspirations in the terms
used in this document. In the official laudation given
it by the organ of its supporters the following occurs:

"Clauses 3 and 4 must be read together. What
they mean is this, that the association in matters of 'common concern' shall be a free one,
not binding Ireland to submit to the decisions
either of the British alone or of a majority of
the States of the Commonwealth of which
Britain is one.

"It is on that footing that an Irish representative would attend meetings of the body
known as the 'Imperial Conference', consisting
of Dominion Premiers and British Cabinet
Ministers to discuss and co-operate in matters
of 'common concern'. That is the footing on
which the Commonwealth States act together
now, and the words within quotation marks at
the end of Clause 4 are taken from what is
known as the Constitutional Resolution passed
at the Imperial Conference of 1917.

"It will be seen that the Commonwealth
States, including Britain are bound to 'consultation' and no more. They are free to take
action 'as their several Governments may
determine'—a partnership based on individual freedom. Ireland would be in the same
position."

Thus, Ireland is by our own free offer, under this document, represented at the Imperial Conference. Our status is taken from a Constitutional Resolution passed at an Imperial Conference. The outlook of the author of the document is bounded entirely by the horizon of the British Empire.

This is not my stand, and at a Conference in London with the British representatives I made it quite clear that Ireland was A MOTHER COUNTRY, with the duties and responsibilities and feelings and devotions of a mother country.

This simple statement had more effect on the British delegates than all the arguments about Dominion status, or all the arguments basing the claim of our historic nation on any new-found idea. Irish nationhood springs from the Irish people, not from any comparison with any other nation, not from any equality—inherent or acquired—with any other nation.

Clause 1 of the document, which states:

> "That the legislative, executive and judicial authority of Ireland shall be derived solely from the people of Ireland,"

is a declaration of rights more suitable to form the basis of the Constitution of a free nation than to be incorporated in a Treaty of Peace between two nations that had been at war.

The opponents of the Treaty were most insistent on the argument that it was Britain (by passing the Treaty through her parliament) who conferred on us the Rights and Powers of the Treaty. But we definitely stipulate for a like British acquiescence in Document No. 2.

That is clear from the clause asking for ratification by the British Parliament. British ratification is a legal thing. It is no worse in one case than in the other. It is no better either. But surely no one recognises any right in Britain to agree or to disagree with that fundamental principle of freedom which concerns the people of Ireland alone.

In fact, the Treaty secures this position. Under the Treaty the English will no longer have any legislative, executive, or judicial authority in Ireland.

All such authority will be vested in the Parliament of Ireland, which alone will have power to make laws for the peace, order, and good government of Ireland.

Clauses 2, 3 and 4 of the document are all a loose paraphrase of the Treaty, dangerous and misleading in their looseness. They read:

(2) "That for purposes of 'common concern' Ireland shall be associated with the States of the British Commonwealth, viz., the Kingdom of Great Britain, the Dominion of Canada, the Commonwealth of Australia, the Dominion of New Zealand, and the Union of South Africa.

(3) "That while voting as an associate, the rights, status, and privileges of Ireland shall be in no respect less than those enjoyed by any of the component States of the British Commonwealth.

(4) "That the matters of 'common concern' shall include Defence, Peace and War, Political Treaties, and all matters now treated as of

'common concern' amongst the States of the British Commonwealth, and that in these matters there shall be between Ireland and the States of the British Commonwealth such concerted action, founded on consultation, as the several Governments may determine."

Under these clauses Ireland would be committed to an association so vague that it might afford grounds for claims by Britain which might give her an opportunity to press for control in Irish affairs as "common concerns", and to use, or to threaten to use, force. The Irish people could not have been asked, and would not have agreed, to commit themselves to anything so vague.

Clause 4 does not mend the matter; it makes it worse, as "common concern" may include anything else besides the things named. In fact, it is common knowledge that there are many common concerns in the inter-dealings between the various States of the Commonwealth.

This is a very vital point. We know that there are many things which the States of the British Commonwealth can afford to regard as "common concerns" which we could not afford so to regard. This is where we must be careful to protect ourselves as best we can against the disadvantages of geographical propinquity. This is where we had to find some form of association which would safeguard us, as far as we could be safeguarded, in somewhat the same degree as the 3,000 miles of ocean safeguards Canada.

And it is obvious that the "association with the British Commonwealth" mentioned in the British

Prime Minister's invitation, which was accepted by Mr. de Valera on behalf of *Dáil Éireann*, meant association of a different kind from that of mere alliance of isolated nations, and now to suggest otherwise is not straightforward.

The question was of an association which would be honourable to Ireland, which would give us full freedom to manage our own affairs, and prevent interference by Britain; which would give the maximum security that this freedom would be observed (and we may be trusted to see that it is so observed), and which would be acceptable to Ireland as recognising her nationhood.

We negotiated from the standpoint of an independent sovereign nation, with a view to finding means of being honourably associated with the British group of nations in a way in which we were not associated with them before the negotiations.

The link which binds that group is a link which binds free nations in a voluntary association. This is what we obtained in the Treaty—freedom within our nation, freedom of association without.

The external association mentioned in Document No. 2 has neither the honesty of complete isolation (a questionable advantage in these days of warring nationalities when it is not too easy for a small nation to stand rigidly alone) nor the strength of free partnership satisfying the different partners. Such external association was not practical politics.

Actually in this regard the terms of the Treaty are less objectionable than the formulas of the document. Restrictions in the Treaty there unquestionably are.

Restrictions in Document No. 2 equally unquestionably there are. *But the Treaty will be operative, and the restrictions must gradually tend to disappear as we go on more and more strongly solidifying and establishing ourselves as a free nation.*

Clause 5. "That in virtue of this association of Ireland with the States of the British Commonwealth citizens of Ireland in any of these States shall not be subject to any disabilities which a citizen of one of the component States of the British Commonwealth would not be subject to, and reciprocally for citizens of these States in Ireland,"

is unintelligible, and does not meet the Irish wish to have some sentimental and racial ties with all the children of our race. The expression "common citizenship" in the Treaty is not ideal, but it is less indefinite, and it does not attempt to confine Ireland's mother claims to the States of the British Commonwealth.

Clause 6. "That for purposes of association, Ireland shall recognise his Britannic Majesty as head of association"

gives the recognition of the British Crown—a recognition which is as precise as any given in the Treaty.

It was after discussion of this clause that Mr. de Valera's alternative oath was produced. That oath, which has already been published, was incorporated in a document submitted to the British by the Irish delegation. It reads as follows:

"I do swear to bear true faith and allegiance to the Constitution of Ireland and to the Treaty of Association of Ireland with the British Commonwealth of Nations, and to recognise the King of Great Britain as head of the Associated States."

It was explained at the *Dáil* debate by one of the foremost anti-Treatyites that the King of Great Britain could be regarded as a managing director, the explanation being that in these modern days industrial concerns were amalgamating and entering into agreements, etc.

The King of Great Britain would then occupy the same relative position towards the Associated States as a managing director occupied towards associated businesses. Whereupon it was very wisely pointed out by a journalist who was listening to the debate that a managing director is one who manages and directs. After all, whatever we may say of royal prerogatives, or anything of that kind, no modern democratic nation is managed and directed by one ruler.

Plain people will not be impressed by this managing director nonsense. Plain people will see no difference between these oaths.

We must always rely upon our own strength to keep the freedom we have obtained and to make it secure. And the constitutional status of Canada, defined in the Treaty, gives us stronger assurance of our immunity from interference by Britain than the indefinite clauses in Document No. 2.

These clauses have nothing effective to back them.

They have practically all the disadvantages of the Treaty. It is too uncertain to have our future relationship based on "ifs" and "unless" and terms like "so far as our resources permit". These attempts at improvement are nothing but dangerous friction spots which it is the interest of Ireland to avoid.

Much has been said by the opponents of the Treaty about "buttressing up the British Empire". All these defence clauses in Document No. 2 are open to exactly the same attack. Under these clauses we could not assist an Indian or Egyptian craft that happened to get into Irish waters. These countries are at war with Britain, and we should be bound by our proffered agreement to help Britain.

Under the Treaty we should have a representative on the League of Nations (if we approved of a League of Nations), and that representative would have a real power to prevent aggression against Egypt and India.

To deal with Clauses 7 and 10 together, these clauses have reference to the matter of defence, and to the ordinary observer there is little difference between them and the clauses of the Treaty covering the same subject.

The Treaty secures that the harbours at certain ports can be used only for purposes of commmon defence, and not for any purpose of interfering with Irish freedom (and, again, we may be trusted to ensure that this shall be so).

There is one other thing under these clauses that I should like to explain from my own knowledge of how the matter arose. The British representatives made it quite clear to us that the British people could not, or would not, for the sake of their own safety, allow any Irish Government to build submarines. Document No. 2 concedes this British claim fully. Britain does not mind if we build a dreadnought or two, a battleship or two. One submarine would be a greater menace to her than these. Document No. 2, therefore, gives way to her on the only point that really matters. Such a concession to British necessity, real or supposed, is nothing but dishonesty. Let us agree, if need be, that we shall not build submarines; but don't let us pretend that we are doing it from any motive other than the real motive.

The remaining clauses seem nothing but a repetition of the clauses of the Treaty, with only such slight verbal alterations as no one but a factionist looking for means of making mischief would have thought it worth while to have risked wrecking the Treaty for.

It is fair criticism that the Treaty contains obsolete phraseology no longer suited to the status of freedom and equality of the States of the British Commonwealth and out of touch with the realities of our freedom. But phraseology does not alter the fact of our freedom, and we have the right and will exercise the right, to use a form of words to secure an interpretation more in accordance with the facts.

As an improvement on the Treaty Document No. 2 is not honest. It may be more dictatorial in language. It does not contain in principle a "greater reconciliation with Irish national aspirations". It merely attaches a fresh label to the same parcel, or, rather, a label written, on purpose, illegibly in the hope of making belief that the parcel is other than it is.

THE PROOF OF SUCCESS
What the Rising of 1916 did
Disunion Danger

I reland is an ancient nation which from earliest times had a distinct civilization. What made Ireland what she was was her people living within the whole island as a separate and distinct community, or nation, by virtue of a common system of law and culture and traditions and ways of life and not depending upon any particular political constitutions. While this lasted strangers who came were absorbed, and the national ways were not interfered with, and were such, by their attractiveness, as to enable strangers to become Irish easily and thoroughly.

Then came English interference, and her policy of robbery and exploitation, and when she had "conquered" us sufficiently she began to carry out her policy—to use us to feed and enrich herself. But having a complete nationhood of our own, which Britain had to acknowledge or to trample out of existence, and having a social system which suited us, and which gave our people security in all their rights and privileges, England found the execution of her policy, though helped by our geographical propinquity, a less easy task in Ireland than in her colonies, where there was no separate nationhood and no difference of social polity.

England's idea was to make Ireland an English province. For her purposes Irish civilization was to be completely blotted out. The Gael was to go. Our lands were to be confiscated and given to aliens. Our industries were to be effectively destroyed. Everything that tended to remind us of the past, everything that tended to retain our Irish outlook, everything that helped to keep us a distinct people, everything that tended to keep alive in us our memories of our Gaelic civilization and of our Irish nationality, freedom, and prosperity, was to be obliterated.

Her method even then was to divide and rule, setting chief against chief, as later she set religion against religion.

This policy could not succeed while we had a land system by which men's rights in the land were secure and impregnable. By means of wholesale commandeering the land was taken from the people, and the feudal system of tenure, a system admirably suited for the purpose of enslavement, was imposed. The free men of Ireland, whose rights had been rooted in the soil, became the tenants, the serfs, of the usurpers, and were completely at the mercy of their new masters, the landlords, who joined with the enemy in the policy of robbing, exploiting, and exterminating the Irish people.

When England had succeeded in uprooting the old Irish system of land tenure under which everyone securely enjoyed land to cultivate and common rights of grazing, she had taken the biggest step in our subjection. It was only in so far as it attempted to reverse that subjection that the land campaign of the Davitt period was justified.

Some historian has yet to take up this aspect of the land struggle and discover a national spirit seeking to manifest itself in apparently strange ways. Were it not for this the killing of landlords would have been murder. The people undoubtedly regarded it in this way. The landlords were the agents who had taken away the liberties of the common folk, and the common folk hit at the agent whom they recognised as the common enemy.

They took first things first. They did the job which was immediately to their hands. In our generation we have no longer to shoot landlords, for landlords as they were known have mostly gone. In the same way we hope that the next generation will have no necessity to shoot an enemy, for the enemy will have gone.

In furtherance of the same policy the suppression of our industries was also necessary if Britain's desire was to be realised. It was doubly necessary. Our manufacturers competed too successfully with hers, and it was to be our privilege to exist, not as an industrial people, but for the purpose of providing England with an abundance of food.

The destruction of our democratic Gaelic social system, the discouragement, the prohibition of all enterprise, leaving us only a slave life on the land, and the imposition upon us of an alien language, alien laws, alien ideas, made our subjugation complete. Our economic subjection was necessary that we might serve Britain's purposes. Our spiritual subjection was no less necessary that we might learn to forget our former national and economic freedom and acquiesce and grow passive in our servitude.

And we learned our lesson. We forgot our freedom. We forgot our language. We forgot our own native Irish ways. We forgot our Irish love and veneration for things of the mind and character, our pride in learning, in the arts for which we had been famous, in military skill, in athletic prowess, in all which had been our glory from the days of Cormac MacArt and St. Patrick and before them.

We became the degraded and feeble imitators of our tyrants. English fashions, English material tastes and customs were introduced by the landlord class or adopted by them, and by a natural process they came to be associated in the minds of our people with gentility. The outward sign of a rise in the social scale became the extent to which we cast off everything which distinguished us as Irish and the success with which we imitated the enemy who despised us.

And slavery still exists.

To-day in Ireland, although through improved economic conditions, which have been world-wide and in which it was not possible altogether to prevent us sharing, helped by a better living on the land, bought very dearly by the purchase back again of a great part of our country from those who had never any right to it, we have been lifted out of the worst slough of destitution; although we have been turning our eyes towards the light of liberty and learning to lift our heads again as Irish men and Irish women with a land of our own, and with traditions and hopes of which no nation need feel ashamed, yet still from east to west, from north to south, we are soaked, saturated, and stupefied with the English outlook.

Only slowly, laboriously, do we turn in our chains and struggle to free ourselves from the degrading lie that what is English is necessarily respectable, and what is Irish, low and mean. Even at this moment when our daily papers and our weekly papers are writing of our newly-won freedom and rejoicing over our national hopes, they continue to announce in their leading columns the movements of English society and the births and marriages of upper-class English nonentities.

But by the completeness with which England converted us into hewers of wood and drawers of water, she in the end defeated her own purpose.

Feebly resisting at the moments when we were less completely crushed, when a brief interval came between the long periods of starvation, when we had a moment in which we could reflect upon our condition, we gradually awoke to the cause of our miseries, and we grew to learn if we would be economically free we must be nationally free, and if we would be spiritually free we must be nationally free.

The coming and the presence of the English had deprived us of life and liberty. Their ways were not our ways. Their interests and their purposes meant our destruction. We must turn back again the wheels of that infamous machine which was destroying us. We must get the English out of Ireland.

Our efforts at first were naturally timid, and they were often futile because we were too much concerned with the political side—confused in this by the example of England where nationality was always expressed that way, and was principally a matter of political organisation.

Repeal of the Union was little more than a cry gaining what real strength it had from the more vigorous hostility of the Young Ireland movement, which revived our old literature, which recovered Irish history, and spread a new spirit. That spirit was not wholly martial, but what Irishman will say to-day that it was not beneficial, even so?

The Fenians came and once and for all raised the banner of Ireland's freedom, with a definite military policy which, though unsuccessful at the time, had its full effect in bringing before men's minds the real road to Irish salvation.

The Fenian idea left a torch behind it with which Tom Clarke and Seán MacDermott kindled the fires of Easter Week, and, though seemingly quenched, these were soon blazing brightly again at Solohead, at Clonfin, at Macroom, at Dublin, at many a place in Clare, in Mayo, and Monaghan, and Donegal during the recent struggle.

After the Fenians, years of death again, while famine raged over the land, till Parnell emerged to struggle for independence under the name of Home Rule which, though accompanied by the social and economic revolt of Davitt's national land policy, was bringing us back again to the dangerous idea of seeking freedom by means of some form of political weapon.

The weakness inherent in Parnell's policy was obviated by his intense personal hostility to the English.

He never forgot the end in the means. But it lost that saving protection when it fell into the hands of those who succeeded him and who, in the lotus-like atmosphere of the Westminster Parliament, forgot the national spirit and lost touch with the minds and feelings of their countrymen.

The collapse came when in the hands of weaker men the national effort became concentrated at the foreign parliament on English political lines. The methods adopted by the parliamentarians, the forum they had chosen, made their crumbling an easy matter, and from the English point of view it greatly helped division in their ranks, and with division came the inevitable dissipation of energy.

We would have an identical situation to-day had we chosen the same methods and fought on the same battlefield for the last five years. In that parliamentary period, however, the people at home were growing in national consciousness and in strength and courage. The Gaelic revival and the learning of our national tongue were teaching a new national self-respect. We recalled the immortal tales of our ancient heroes, and we began to look to a future in which we could have a proud, free, distinct nation worthy of the past.

We learned that what we wanted was not a political form of Home Rule or any other kind or form of Home Rule, but a revival of Gaelic life and ways. Economic thought and study showed us that the poverty which afflicted us came from the presence of the English and their control over us; had come from landlordism and the drain of English taxation, the neglect of Irish resources, and the obstruction to Irish industries by the domination of the English Parliament. And we saw that we must manage these things for ourselves. And, besides the hope of material emancipation, we grew to think of love of our land, and all that it had given us and had still to give us, and what we could make of it when it was our own once more. And we became filled with a patriotic fervour before which, when the time came, force would prove impotent. The expression of this new hope and new courage manifested itself in the Easter Week Rising.

The leaven of the old Fenianism had been at work in our midst. Tom Clarke, a member of the old Fenian Brotherhood, came out from jail after sixteen years' penal servitude to take up the work where he had left it off.

Seán MacDermott, tramping through Ireland, preached the Fenian gospel of a freedom which must be fought for, enrolled recruits, and, by his pure patriotism and lovable unselfish character, inspired all with whom he came in contact to emulate him and to be worthy of his teaching.

Our army was in existence again. It was not brought into being, as is wrongfully supposed, by the example of Carson's recruiting in North-East Ulster. It needed no such example. It was already in being—the old Irish Republican Brotherhood in fuller force.

But England's manufactured resistance in the North-East enabled our soldiers to come out into the open, with the advantage in 1916 of a Rising starting unexpectedly from the streets instead of from underground. England was unable or unwilling to interfere with her own Orange instruments, and she did not dare, therefore, to suppress ours.

Armed resistance was the indispensable factor in our struggle for freedom. It was never possible for us to be militarily strong, but we could be strong enough to make England uncomfortable (and strong enough to make England too uncomfortable). While she explains the futility of force (by others) it is the only argument she listens to. For ourselves it had that practical advantage, but it was above all other things the expression of our separate nationhood.

Unless we were willing to fight for our Nation, even without any certainty of success, we acquiesced in the doctrine of our national identity with England. It embodied, too, for us the spirit of sacrifice, the maintenance of the ideal, the courage to die for it, so that military efforts were made in nearly every generation. It was a protest, too, against our anglicisation and demoralisation, a challenge of spirit against material power, and as such bore fruit.

The Rising of 1916 was the fruit.

It appeared at the time of the surrender to have failed, but that valiant effort and the martyrdoms which followed it finally awoke the sleeping spirit of Ireland.

It carried into the hearts of the people the flame which had been burning in those who had the vision to see the pit into which we were sinking deeper and deeper and who believed that a conflagration was necessary to reveal to their countrymen the road to national death upon which we were blindly treading.

The banner of Ireland's freedom had been raised and was carried forward. During the Rising the leaders of Easter Week "declared a Republic". But not as a fact. We knew it was not a fact. It was a wonderful gesture—throwing down the gauntlet of defiance to the enemy, expressing to ourselves the complete freedom we aimed at, and for that reason was an inspiration to us.

If the impossible had happened, and the Rising had succeeded, and the English had surrendered and evacuated the country, we would then have been free, and we could then have adopted the republican form of government, or any other form we wished. But the Rising did not succeed as a military venture. And if it had succeeded it would have been the surrender and the evacuation which would have been the proof of our success, not the name for, nor the form of, the government we would have chosen. If we had still a descendant of our Irish Kings left, we would be as free, under a limited monarchy, with the British gone, as under a Republic.

The form of our government is our domestic Irish concern. It does not affect the fact of our national freedom. Our national freedom depends upon the extent to which we reverse the history of the last 700 years, the extent to which we get rid of the enemy and get rid of his control over our material and spiritual life.

FOUR HISTORIC YEARS
The Story of 1914–1918
How Ireland Made her Case Clear

The period from 1914 to 1918 is an important one in the struggle for Irish freedom. It was a transition period. It saw a wholesome and necessary departure from the ideas and methods which had been held and adopted for a generation, and it is a period which is misread by a great many of our people, even by some who helped that departure, and who helped to win the success we have achieved.

The real importance of the Rising of 1916 did not become apparent until 1918. It is not correct to say now that the assertion of the republican principle which was stated by the leaders of the Rising was upheld as the national policy without a break. The declaration of a Republic was really in advance of national thought, and it was only after a period of two years' propaganda that we were actually able to get solidarity on the idea.

The European War, which began in 1914, is now generally recognised to have been a war between two rival empires, an old one and a new, the new becoming such a successful rival of the old, commercially and militarily, that the world-stage was, or was thought to be, not large enough for both.

Germany spoke frankly of her need for expansion, and for new fields of enterprise for her surplus population. England, who likes to fight under a high-sounding title, got her opportunity in the invasion of Belgium. She was entering the war "in defence of the freedom of small nationalities".

America at first looked on, but she accepted the motive in good faith, and she ultimately joined in as the champion of the weak against the strong. She concentrated attention upon the principle of "self-determination" and "the reign of law based upon the consent of the governed".

"Shall," asked President Wilson, "the military power of any nation, or group of nations, be suffered to determine the fortunes of peoples over whom they have no right to rule except the right of force?"

But the most flagrant instance of the violation of this principle did not seem to strike the imagination of President Wilson, and he led the American nation—peopled so largely by Irish men and women who had fled from British oppression—into the battle and to the side of that nation which for hundreds of years had "determined the fortunes" of the Irish people against their wish, and had ruled them, and was still ruling them, by no other right than the right of force.

There were created by the Allied Powers half-a-dozen new Republics as a demonstration of adherence to these principles. At the same time, England's military subjection of Ireland continued. And Ireland was a nation with claims as strong as, or stronger than, those of the other small nations.

This subjugation constituted a mockery of those principles, yet the expression of them before the world as principles for which great nations were willing to pour out their blood and treasure gave us the opportunity to raise again our flag of freedom and to call the attention of the world to the denial of our claim.

We were not pro-German during the war any more than we were pro-Bulgarian, pro-Turk, or anti-French. We were anti-British, pursuing our age-long policy against the common enemy. Not only was this our policy, but it was the policy that any weak nation would have pursued in the same circumstances. We were a weak nation kept in subjection by a stronger one, and we formed and adopted our policy in light of this fact. We remembered that England's difficulty was Ireland's opportunity, and we took advantage of her engagement elsewhere to make a bid for freedom.

The odds between us were for the moment a little less unequal. Our hostility to England was the common factor between Germany and ourselves. We made common cause with France when France was fighting. We made common cause with Spain when Spain was fighting England. We made common cause with the Dutch when the Dutch were fighting England.

It so happened that on this occasion England had put a weapon into our hands against herself. The observation of the world was focused upon the mighty European War. We could call attention to the difference between England's principles as expounded to the world and her practice as against ourselves. We were put into the position of being able to force her to recognise our freedom or to oppress us for proclaiming that simple right.

Our position was our old position. Our aim was our old aim. Our intention was simply to secure liberation from the English occupation and that which it involved.

The Rising expressed our right to freedom. It expressed our determination to have the same liberty of choice in regard to our own destinies as was conceded to Poland or Czecho-Slovakia, or any other of the nations that were emerging as a result of the new doctrines being preached. The Republic which was declared at the Rising of Easter Week, 1916, was Ireland's expression of the freedom she aspired to. It was our way of saying that we wished to challenge Britain's right to dominate us.

Ireland wished to make it clear that she stood for a form of freedom equal to that of any other nation. Other nations claimed freedom, and their claims were conceded. Ireland's claim was no less strong than the claim of any nation. We had as good a right to recognition as Poland has. The position we adopted expressed our repudiation of the British government.

The British form of government was monarchical. In order to express clearly our desire to depart from all British forms, we declared a Republic. We repudiated the British form of government, not because it was monarchical, but because it was British. We would have repudiated the claim of a British Republic to rule over us as definitely as we repudiated the claim of the British monarchy.

Our claim was to govern ourselves, and the expression of the form of government was an answer to the British lie that Ireland was a domestic question. It was a gesture to the world that there could be no confusion about. It was an emphasis of our separate nationhood and a declaration that our ultimate goal was and would continue to be complete independence.

It expressed our departure from the policy of parliamentary strategy at Westminster. That policy had failed, as it was bound to fail. It had two evils involved in it. While claiming rightly to be a distinct nation, we had been acquiescing by our actions in the convenient British doctrine that we were a British province and an integral part of the United Kingdom—an acquiescence which gave Mr. Lloyd George the opportunity to question our right to freedom because for over a hundred years, he said, we had sent representatives to Westminster, and soldiers to fight in every British war.

And it had the evil effect of causing our people to look to England for any ameliorative government, and even for the "gift" of an instalment of freedom, and away from their own country, from themselves, who alone could give to themselves these things. So we sank more and more into subjection during this period, and it was only by a great educational effort that our national consciousness was re-awakened.

We were to learn that freedom was to be secured by travelling along a different road; that instead of it being possible for the English to bestow freedom upon us as a gift (or by means of any Treaty signed or unsigned) that it was their presence alone which denied it to us, and we must make that presence uncomfortable for them, and that the only question between us and them was the terms on which they would clear out and cease their interference with us.

But we started along the new road, the only one that could lead to freedom, at first with faltering steps, half doubtingly looking back at the old paths which had become familiar, where we knew the milestones at which we had been able to shift the burden from one shoulder to another.

The Easter Week Rising pointed out the road. But after that declaration of a Republic and all that it meant of repudiation of Britain, we lapsed into the old way, or took but uncertain steps upon the new one.

When the first by-election after the Rising took place in North Roscommon in 1917, so much had the Republic of Easter Week been forgotten and so little had its teachings yet penetrated to the minds of the people, that, though the candidate was Count Plunkett, whose son had been martyred after the Rising, he was returned only on the ground of his opposition to the Irish Party candidate.

Abstention from attendance at the British Parliament was the indispensable factor in the republican ideal—the repudiation of foreign government. But it was only after his election that the Count declared his intention not to go to Westminster, and the announcement was not received very enthusiastically by some of the most energetic of his supporters.

They had returned a man, it was said, "who did not intend to represent them anywhere". Not only the people, but even some who had been engaged in the Rising hardly grasped the new teaching.

This election and others which followed were not won on the policy of upholding a Republic, but on the challenge it made to the old Irish Party.

There was at this stage no unity of opinion on the policy of abstention among the various elements which formed the opposition, which were joined together only on opposition to the Redmondites. At what was known as "the Plunkett Convention" an effort was made to get all the parts of the opposition united on such a policy but the divergence of opinion was so great that, to avoid a split, it was declared that there should be no greater union than a loose co-operation.

The North Roscommon and the South Longford elections were fought on the basis of this agreement, and there was no definite united policy until the merging of all the sectional organisations with *Sinn Féin* which occurred just prior to the great *Árd-Fheis* of 1917.

At the South Longford election Mr. Joe McGuinness, who was then still in penal servitude, was elected on the cry: "Put him in to get him out." Abstention was put forward, but was so little upheld that he was returned with a majority of only 27.

At the East Clare election, though Mr. de Valera put forward the abstentionist policy and was elected by a large majority, he issued no election address, and at the three elections which followed in South Armagh,

Waterford, and East Tyrone, the abstentionists were defeated.

But the people were becoming educated, and the union of all the various sects and leagues in the big organisation of *Sinn Féin*, as we have seen, defined the national policy as definitely abstentionist.

The Republic of Easter Week had not lived on, as is supposed, supported afresh at each election, and endorsed finally in the General Election of 1918. But the people grew to put their trust in the new policy, and to believe that the men who stood for it would do their best for Ireland, and at the General Election of 1918, fought on the principle of self-determination, they put them in power.

COLLAPSE OF THE TERROR
British Rule's Last Stages
What the Elections Meant

We have seen how in ancient Ireland the people were themselves the guardians of their land, doing all for themselves according to their own laws and customs, as interpreted by the Brehons, which gave them security, prosperity, and national greatness, and how this was upset by the English determination to blot out Irish ways, when came poverty, demoralisation and a false respect for English standards and habits.

The English power to do this rested on military occupation and on economic control. It had the added advantage of social influence operating upon a people weakened and demoralised by the state of dependence into which the English occupation had brought them.

Military resistance was attempted. Parliamentary strategy was tried. The attempts did not succeed. They failed because they did not go to the root of the question.

The real cure had to be started—that the people should recover belief in their own ways and ideas and put them into practice. Secret societies were formed and organised. The Land League came into existence. The Gaelic League came. *Sinn Féin* grew and developed. All these societies did much. But the effort had to be broadened into a national movement to become irresistible. It became irresistible in the Republican movement when it was backed by sufficient military force to prevent the English forces from suppressing the national revival.

The challenge of Easter Week and its sacrifices increased the growing national self-belief. All these things made a resistance against which the English, with their superior forces, pitted themselves in vain.

Ireland's story from 1918 to 1921 may be summed up as the story of a struggle between our determination to govern ourselves and to get rid of British government and the British determination to prevent us from doing either. It was a struggle between two rival Governments, the one an Irish Government resting on the will of the people and the other an alien Government depending for its existence upon military force—the one gathering more and more authority, the other steadily losing ground and growing ever more desperate and unscrupulous.

All the history of the three years must be read in the light of that fact.

Ireland had never acquiesced in government by England. Gone for ever were policies which were a tacit admission that a foreign Government could bestow freedom, or a measure of freedom, upon a nation which had never surrendered its national claim.

We could take our freedom. We would set up a Government of our own and defend it. We would take the government out of the hands of the foreigner, who had no right to it, and who could exercise it only by force.

A war was being waged by England and her Allies in defence, it was said, of the freedom of small nationalities, to establish in such nations "the reign of law based upon the consent of the governed". We, too, proposed to establish in Ireland "the reign of law based upon the consent of the governed".

At the General Election of 1918 the Irish Parliamentary Party was repudiated by the Irish people by a majority of over 70 per cent. And they gave authority to their representatives to establish a National Government. The National Government was set up in face of great difficulties. *Dáil Éireann* came into being. British law was gradually superseded. *Sinn Féin* Courts were set up. Commissions were appointed to investigate and report upon the national resources of the country with a view to industrial revival. Land courts were established which settled long-standing disputes. Volunteer police were enrolled. (They were real police, to protect life and property, not military police and police spies to act with an enemy in attacks upon both.) A loan of £400,000 was raised. The local governing bodies of the country were directed, inspected, and controlled by *Dáil Éireann*. We established a bank to finance societies which wished to acquire land.

But these facts must be concealed.

At first the British were content to ridicule the new Government. Then, growing alarmed at its increasing authority, attempts were made to check its activities by wholesale political arrests.

The final phase of the struggle had begun.

In the first two years all violence was the work of the British armed forces who in their efforts at suppression murdered fifteen Irishmen and wounded nearly 400 men, women, and children. Meetings were broken up everywhere. National newspapers were suppressed. Over 1,000 men and women were arrested for political offences, usually of the most trivial nature. Seventy-seven of the national leaders were deported.

No police were killed during these two years. The only disorder and bloodshed were the work of the British forces.

These forces were kept here or sent here by the British Government to harass the development of Irish self-government. They were intended to break up the national organisation. They were intended to goad the people into armed resistance. Then they would have the excuse which they hoped for. Then they could use wholesale violence, and end up by the suppression of the national movement.

But they did not succeed.

In the municipal elections in January, 1920, the people answered afresh. In the rural elections in May and June, 1920, the people repeated their answer. The people supported their leaders and their policy by even larger majorities than the majorities given by the election in November, 1918.

The British Government now decided that a greater effort was needed. The moment had come for a final desperate campaign.

The leading London newspaper, *The Times*, declared in a leading article of November 1st, 1920, that it was "now generally admitted" that a deliberate policy of violence had been "conceived and sanctioned in advance by an influential section of the Cabinet".

But to admit such a policy was impossible. It was necessary to conceal the real object of the Reign of Terror, for the destruction of the national movement, which was about to begin.

First, the ground had to be prepared. In August, 1920, a law was passed "to restore law and order in Ireland". This law in reality abolished all law in Ireland, and left the lives and property of the people defenceless before the British forces. It facilitated and protected—and was designed to facilitate and protect—those forces in the task they were about to undertake. Coroners' inquests were prohibited, so that no inquiry could be made into the acts of violence contemplated. National newspapers, that could not be trusted to conceal the facts and to publish only supplied information, were suppressed. Newspaper correspondents were threatened.

The ground prepared, special instruments had to be selected. "It is," said the London *Times*, "common knowledge that the Black and Tans were recruited from ex-soldiers for a rough and dangerous task." This "rough and dangerous task", which had been "conceived and sanctioned" by the British Cabinet, was to be carried out under three headings. Certain leading men, and Irish Army officers, were to be murdered, their names being entered on a list "for definite clearance". All who worked for or supported the national movement were to be imprisoned, and the general population was to be terrorised into submission.

A special newspaper, *The Weekly Summary,* was circulated amongst the Crown Forces to encourage them in their "rough and dangerous task". As an indication of its intention it invited them in an early number "to make an appropriate hell" in Ireland.

Excuses, for the purpose of concealment, had to be invented. The public had to be prepared for the coming campaign. Mr. Lloyd George in a speech in Carnarvon, October 7, 1920, spoke of the Irish Republican Army as "a real murder gang". We began to hear of "steps necessary to put down a murderous conspiracy". "We have got murder by the throat," said Mr. Lloyd George.

The "murders" were the legitimate acts of self-defence which had been forced upon the Irish people by English aggression. After two years of forbearance, we had begun to defend ourselves and the life of our nation. We did not initiate the war, nor were we allowed to select the battleground. When the British Government, as far as lay in its power, deprived the Irish people of arms, and employed every means to prevent them securing arms, and made it a criminal (in large areas a capital) offence to carry arms, and, at the same time, began and carried out a brutal and murderous campaign against them and against their National Government, they deprived themselves of any excuse for their violence and of any cause of complaint against the Irish people for the means they took for their protection.

For all the acts of violence committed in Ireland from 1916 to 1921 England, and England alone, is responsible. She willed the conflict and fixed the form it was to take.

On the Irish side it took the form of disarming the attackers. We took their arms and attacked their strongholds. We organised our army and met the armed patrols and military expeditions which were sent against us in the only possible way. We met them by an organised and bold guerilla warfare. But this was not enough. If we were to stand up against the powerful military organisation arrayed against us something more was necessary than a guerilla war in which small bands of our warriors, aided by their knowledge of the country, attacked the larger forces of the enemy and reduced their numbers. England could always reinforce her army. She could replace every soldier that she lost.

But there were others indispensable for her purposes which were not so easily replaced. To paralyse the British machine it was necessary to strike at individuals. Without her spies England was helpless. It was only by means of their accumulated and accumulating knowledge that the British machine could operate.

Without their police throughout the country, how could they find the men they "wanted"? Without their criminal agents in the capital, how could they carry out that "removal" of the leaders that they considered essential for their victory? Spies are not so ready to step into the shoes of their departed confederates as are soldiers to fill up the front line in honourable battle. And even when the new spy stepped into the shoes of the old one, he could not step into the old one's knowledge.

The most potent of these spies were Irishmen enlisted in the British service and drawn from the

small farmer and labourer class. Well might every
Irishman at present ask himself if we were doing a
wrong thing in getting rid of the system which was
responsible for bringing these men into the ranks of
the opponents of their own race.

We struck at individuals, and by so doing we cut
their lines of communication and we shook their
morale. And we conducted the conflict, difficult as it
was, with the unequal terms imposed by the enemy,
as far as possible, according to the rules of war. Only
the armed forces and the spies and criminal agents of
the British Government were attacked. Prisoners of
war were treated honourably and considerately, and
were released after they had been disarmed.

On the English side they waged a sort of war, but
did not respect the laws and usages of war. When our
soldiers fell into their hands they were "murderers",
to be dealt with by the bullet or the rope of the hang-
man. They were dealt with mostly by the bullet.
Strangely enough, when it became the "law" that prisoners attempting to escape should be shot, a considerably larger number of our prisoners "attempted to
escape" than when the greatest penalty to be expected was recapture.

The fact was that when the men whose names were
"upon the list" were identified at once, they were shot
at once. When they were identified during a raid, they
were taken away and shot "while attempting to escape".
Or they were brought to Dublin Castle or other place of
detention and questioned under torture, and on refus-
ing to give information were murdered because they
"revolted", "seized arms", and "attacked their guards".

For these murders no members of the British forces were brought to justice. The perpetrators were but "enforcing the law"—"restoring law and order in Ireland...". No matter how damaging the evidence, the prisoners were invariably acquitted. Necessarily so. They were but carrying out the duties which they had been specially hired at a very high rate of pay to execute.

To excuse the terrible campaign, the world began to hear of "reprisals", "the natural outbreaks of the rank and file". A campaign which could no longer be concealed had to be excused—a campaign in which sons were murdered before the eyes of their mothers—in which fathers were threatened with death and done to death because they would not tell the whereabouts of their sons—in which men were made to crawl along the streets, and were taken and stripped and flogged, and sent back naked to their homes—in which towns and villages and homes were burned, and women and children left shivering in the fields.

Excuses were necessary for such deeds, and we began to hear of "some hitting back" by "the gallant men who are doing their duty in Ireland". The London *Westminster Gazette* of October 27, 1920, published a message from their own correspondent at Cork which gives an instance of the way in which these "gallant men" performed their "duty":

"A motor lorry of uniformed men, with blackened faces, arrived in Lixane from the Ballybunion district. Before entering the village they pulled up at the house of a farmer named

Patrick McElligott. His two sons were pulled outside the door in night attire in a downpour of rain, cruelly beaten with the butt ends of rifles and kicked. The party then proceeded to the house of a young man named Stephen Grady, where they broke in the door. Grady escaped in his night attire through the back window. Searchlights were turned on him, but he made good his escape through the fields. His assistant, named Nolan, was knocked unconscious on the floor with a rifle, and subsequently brought outside the door almost nude and a tub of water poured over him. The party then broke into the room where Miss Grady and her mother were sleeping, pulled Miss Grady out on the road and cut her hair."

The account tells of the burning of the creamery and of further escapades of the "gallant men" on their return through the village.

An instance symbolic of the fight, of the devotion and self-sacrifice on the one side, and the brutish insensibility on the other, was the murder on October 25, 1920, of young Willie Gleeson, of Finaghy, Co. Tipperary. Officers of the British Army Intelligence Staff raided the house of his father, looking for another of his sons. Hearing his father threatened with death if he would not (or could not) disclose where his son was, Willie came from his bed and offered himself in place of his father. The offer was accepted, and he was taken out into the yard and shot dead.

On the same night the same party (presumably) murdered Michael Ryan, of Curraghduff, Co. Tipperary, in the presence of his sister. Ryan was lying ill in bed with pneumonia and the sister described the scene in which one officer held a candle over the bed to give better light to his comrade in carrying out the deed. Such "reprisals" could not be explained as "a severe hitting back", and a new excuse was forthcoming. They were suggested as a just retribution falling upon murderers.

Mr. Lloyd George was "firmly convinced that the men who are suffering in Ireland are the men who are engaged in a murderous conspiracy". At the London Guildhall he announced that the police were "getting the right men". As it became more and more difficult to conceal the truth the plea of unpremeditation was dropped, and the violence was explained as legitimate acts of self-defence.

But when the Terror, growing evermore violent, and, consequently, ever more ineffective, failed to break the spirit of the Irish people—failed as it was bound to fail—concealment was no longer possible, and the true explanation was blurted out when Mr. Lloyd George and Mr. Bonar Law declared that their acts were necessary to destroy the authority of the Irish National Government which "has all the symbols and all the realities of government".

When such a moment had been reached, there was only one course left open for the British Prime Minister—to invite the Irish leaders, the "murderers", and "heads of the murder gang" to discuss with him terms of peace. The invitation was:

73

"To discuss terms of peace—to ascertain how the association of Ireland with the community of nations known as the British Empire may best be reconciled with Irish national aspirations."

We all accepted that invitation.

PARTITION ACT'S FAILURE
Unity as a Means to
Full Freedom

While the Terror in Ireland was at its height the British Cabinet passed the Government of Ireland Act, 1920, better known as the Partition Act. It is not quite clear what was in the minds of the British Prime Minister and his Cabinet in passing this measure. Nobody representing any Irish constituency voted for it in the British Parliament.

Nationalist Ireland took advantage of its election machinery only to repudiate the Act and to secure a fresh mandate from the people. Otherwise the Act was completely ignored by us. In the Six Counties almost one-fourth of the candidates were returned in non-recognition of the Act, while Sir James Craig himself said, they (he and his friends) accepted the parliament conferred upon them by the Act only as "a great sacrifice".

The Act was probably intended for propaganda purposes. It might do to allay world criticism—to draw attention away from British violence for a month or two longer. At the end of that period Ireland would, it was hoped, have been terrorised into submission.

That desired end gained, a chastened nation would accept the crumb of freedom offered by the Act. Britain, with her idea of the principles of self-determination satisfied, would be able to present a bold front again before the world.

There was, probably, too, an understanding with the Orange leaders. The act entrenched them (or appeared to) within the Six Counties. No doubt, both the British and Orange leaders had it in mind that if a bigger settlement had ultimately to be made with Ireland, a position was secured from which they could bargain.

In any "settlement" the North-East was to be let down gently by the British Government. Pampered for so long they had learned to dictate to and to bully the nation to which they professed to be loyal. They must be treated with tact in regard to any change of British policy towards Ireland.

They had been very useful. When the Partition Act failed to achieve what was expected of it, and when the Terror failed, a real settlement with Ireland became inevitable. The North-East was now no longer useful to prevent Irish freedom, but she could be useful in another way. She could buttress Britain's determination that, while agreeing to our freedom, Ireland must remain associated with the British group of nations. Britain's reason for insisting upon this association is that she believes it necessary for her own national safety.

Were Britain to go to that, her maximum, it could be represented *to us* that the North-East would never acquiesce in more. It could be represented *to them* that in such a settlement they would be preserving that which they professed to have at heart, the sentimental tie with the Empire to which they were supposed to be attached.

North-East Ulster had been created and maintained not for her own advantage, but to uphold Britain's policy. Everything was done to divide the Irish people and to keep them apart. If we could be made to believe we were the enemies of each other, the real enemy would be overlooked. In this policy Britain has been completely successful. She petted a minority into becoming her agents with the double advantage of maintaining her policy and keeping us divided.

Long ago, setting chief against chief served its purpose in providing the necessary excuse for declaring our lands forfeited. Plantations by Britain's agents followed. The free men of Ireland became serfs on the lands of their fathers. Ireland, by these means, was converted into a British beef farm, and when by force of change and circumstances these means became outworn the good results were continued by setting religion against religion and then worker against worker.

If we were to be kept in subjection we must be kept apart. One creed, the creed of the minority, was selected to be used for the purpose of division and domination. "A Protestant garrison was in possession of the land, magistracy, and power of the country, holding that property under the tenure of British power and supremacy, and ready at every instant to crush the rising of the conquered." Manufactures had become discouraged and destroyed throughout the greater part of Ireland. This was the outcome of British jealousy, and was in accordance with Britain's settled policy towards Ireland.

A revival took place during Grattan's Parliament, partly owing to the war conditions prevailing, but also due to the protection given to industry by the Parliament. The good effect lived on for a little (only for a little) after the Union. A deep depression took place in agriculture at the beginning of the nineteenth century, and agriculture had become the sole industry of the Catholic population. This gave the opportunity to point to the supposed superior qualities of the Protestant industrial worker and to prejudice him still further against his Catholic countrymen.

But North-East Ulster had not flourished and could not flourish under a policy devised for English purposes. It has resulted only in a general decline in prosperity throughout the whole country, only in an uneconomic distribution of the disappearing wealth, only, by contrast, in an appearance of prosperity in one section of the people as compared with the other.

The population of Ulster has decreased by one-third since the 'forties. It is true that the population of Belfast has increased in the last two generations, but the two counties of Antrim and Down, in which Belfast is situated, contain to-day fewer people than before the Famine of 1846-8. Emigration has steadily increased. The number of emigrants from Down and Antrim, including Belfast, has in the last ten years more than doubled that of the preceding ten years.

If there has been any gain in wealth in North-East Ulster as compared with the rest of Ireland, it is obvious that the wealth has not percolated through to the workers for their weal. They, too, like their poor countrymen in Connemara, have to seek better economic conditions in America and other countries.

Capitalism has come, not only to serve Britain's purpose by keeping the people divided, but, by setting worker against worker, it has profited by exploiting both. It works on religious prejudices. It represents to the Protestant workman any attempt by the Catholic workman to get improved conditions as the cloak for some insidious political game.

Such a policy—the policy of divide and rule, and the opportunity it gives for private economic oppression—could bring nothing but evil and hardship to the whole of Ireland.

If Britain had not maintained her interference and carried out her policy the planters would have become absorbed in the old Irish way. Protestant and Catholic would have learned to live side by side in amity and co-operation. Freedom would have come long ago. Prosperity would have come with it. Ireland would have taken her rightful place in the world, the place due to her by her natural advantages, the place due to her by the unique character of her people.

Who will not say that from Britain's policy it is the North-East which has suffered most? She has lost economically and spiritually. She has suffered in reputation by allowing herself to be used for anti-national purposes. She might have gained real wealth as a sturdy and independent section of the population. She exchanged it for a false ascendancy over her countrymen, which has brought her nothing but dishonour. A large portion of her fair province has lost all its native distinctiveness. It has become merely an inferior Lancashire. Who would visit Belfast or Lisburn or Lurgan to see the Irish people at home? That is the unhappy fate of the North-East. It is neither English nor Irish. But what of the future? The North-East is about to get back into the pages of Irish history. Being no longer useful to prevent Irish freedom, forces of persuasion and pressure are embodied in the Treaty of Peace, which has been signed by the Irish and British Plenipotentiaries, to induce North-East Ulster to join in a united Ireland.

If they join in, the Six Counties will certainly have a generous measure of local autonomy. If they stay out, the decision of the Boundary Commission, arranged for in Clause 12, would be certain to deprive "Ulster" of Fermanagh and Tyrone.

Shorn of those counties, she would shrink into insignificance. The burdens and financial restrictions of the Partition Act will remain on North-East Ulster if she decides to stay out. No lightening of these burdens or restrictions can be effected by the English Parliament without the consent of Ireland. Thus, union is certain. The only question for North-East Ulster is—*How soon?*

And that *how soon* may depend largely upon us, upon ourselves of Nationalist Ireland. What if the Orangemen were to get new allies in place of the departing British?

The opposition of Mr. de Valera and his followers to the Treaty is already prejudicing the chances of unity. As the division in our own ranks has become more apparent, the attitude of Sir James Craig has hardened. The organised ruffianism of the North-East has broken out afresh. British troops have been hurried to Ulster. The evacuation has been suspended.

So long as there are British troops in Ireland so long will the Orangemen hold out. While they can look to Britain they will not turn towards the South. They are not giving up their ascendancy without a struggle. Any Irishman who creates and supports division amongst us is standing in the way of a united Ireland. While the Treaty is threatened the British will remain. While the British remain the North-East will keep apart. Just as the evil British policy of *divide and rule* is about to end for ever, we are threatened with a new division, jeopardising the hopes of Irish rule.

No geographical barrier could have succeeded in dividing Ireland. The four or six counties are not counties of Great Britain; they are counties of Ireland. While Britain governed Ireland the North-East could remain apart, she giving allegiance where we gave revolt. Once England surrenders her right to govern us (as she has done under the Treaty) she surrenders her power to divide us. With the British gone the incentive to division is gone.

The fact of union is too strong to be interfered with without the presence of the foreigner bent on dividing us. With the British gone the Orangeman loses that support which alone made him strong enough to keep his position of domination and isolation. Without British support he becomes what he is, one of a minority in the Irish Nation. His rights are the same as those of every Irishman, but he has no rights other than those.

But Britain leaves behind a formidable legacy in the *partition of view*. That is there and it has to be dealt with. It is for us, to whom union is an article of our national faith, to deal with it.

Once the British are gone, I believe we can win our countrymen to allegiance to our common country. Let us convince them of our good will towards them. The first way of doing this is *unity among ourselves*.

We have the task before us to impregnate our northern countrymen with the national outlook. We have a million Protestant Irishmen to convert out of our small population of four-and-a-half millions. Is not that incentive enough to cause us to join together to win a far greater victory than ever we got against the British? If we could have won that victory, there would have been no enemy to vanquish.

The tendency of the sentiment in the North-East, when not interfered with, was national, and in favour of freedom and unity. In that lies our hope.

It is this serious internal problem which argues for the attainment of the final steps of freedom by evolution rather than by force—to give time to the North-East to learn to revolve in the Irish orbit and to get out of the orbit of Great Britain—in fact, internal association with Ireland, external association with Great Britain.

In acquiescing in a peace which involved some postponement of the fulfilment of our national sentiment, by agreeing to some association of our Irish nation with the British nations, we went a long way towards meeting the sentiment of the North-East in its supposed attachment to Great Britain. With such association Britain will have no ground (nor power) for interference, and the North-East no genuine cause for complaint.

Had we been able to establish a Republic at once (we are all now agreed that that was not possible), we would have had to use our resources to coerce North-East Ulster into submission. Will anyone contend that such coercion, if it had succeeded, would have had the lasting effects which conversion on our side and acquiescence on theirs will produce?

The North-East has to be nationalised. Union must come first, unity first as a means to full freedom. Our freedom then will be built on the unshakable foundation of a united people, united in every way, in economic co-operation, and in national outlook.

I have emphasised our desire for national unity above all things. I have stated our desire to win the North-East for Ireland. We mean to do our best in a peaceful way, and if we fail the fault will not be ours.

The freedom we have secured may unquestionably be incomplete. But it is the nearest approach to an absolutely independent and unified Ireland which we can achieve amongst ourselves at the present moment. It certainly gives us the best foothold for final progress.

Let us not waste our energies brooding over *the more we might have got*. Let us look upon *what we have got*. It is a measure of freedom with which we can make an actual, living Ireland when left to our selves. Let us realise that the free Ireland obtained by the Treaty is the greatest common measure of freedom obtainable now, and the most pregnant for future development.

The freedom we have got gives us scope for all that we can achieve by the most strenuous united effort of the present generation to rebuild Ireland.

Can we not all join together to save the Irish ideal—freedom and unity—and to make it a reality?

WHY BRITAIN
SOUGHT IRISH PEACE
Her Failure to Subjugate Us
Making of Treaty

P eace with Ireland, or a good case for further, and what would undoubtedly have been more intensive, war, had become a necessity to the British Cabinet. Politicians of both the great historic parties in Britain had become united in the conviction that it was essential for the British to put themselves right with the world. Referring to the peace offer which Mr. Lloyd George, on behalf of his Cabinet and Parliament, had made to Mr. de Valera in July, 1921 (an offer which was not acceptable to the Irish people) Mr. Churchill said on September 24th at Dundee: "This offer is put forward, not as the offer of a party government confronted by a formidable opposition and anxious to bargain for the Irish vote, but with the united sanction of both the historic parties in the State, and, indeed, all parties. It is a national offer."

Yes. It was a national offer, representing the necessity of the British to clean their Irish slate. The Premiers of the Free Nations of the British Commonwealth were in England fresh from their people. They were able to express the views of their people. The Washington Conference was looming ahead. Mr. Lloyd George's Cabinet had its economic difficulties at home. Their relationships with foreign countries were growing increasingly unhappy, the recovery of world opinion was becoming—in fact, had become—indispensable. Ireland must be disposed of by means of a "generous" peace. If Ireland refused that settlement, we could be shown to be irreconcilables. Then, Britain would again have a free hand for whatever further actions were necessary "to restore law and order" in a country that would not accept the responsibility of doing so for itself.

This movement by the British Cabinet did not indicate any real change of heart on the part of Britain towards Ireland. Any stirrings of conscience were felt only by a minority. This minority was largely the same minority that had been opposed to Britain's intervention in the European War. They were the peaceful group of the English people that is averse from bloodshed on principle, no matter for what purpose, or by whom, carried out. They were opposed to the killing we had to do in self-defence quite as much as they were opposed to the aggressive killing of our people by the various British agents sent here. These pacifists were almost without any political power and had very little popular support.

Peace had become necessary. It was not because Britain repented in the very middle of her Black and Tan terror. It was not because she could not subjugate us before world conscience was awakened and was able to make itself felt. "The progress of the coercive attempts made by the Government have proved in a high degree disappointing," said Lord Birkenhead, frankly, in the British House of Lords on August 10.

What was the position on each side? Right was on our side. World sympathy was on our side (passive sympathy, largely). We had shown a mettle that was a fair indication of what we could do again if freedom were denied us. We were united; we had taken out of the hands of the enemy a good deal of government. We knew it would be no easy matter for him to recover his lost ground in that regard. We had prevented the enemy so far from defeating us.

We had not, however, succeeded in getting the government entirely into our hands, and we had not succeeded in beating the British out of Ireland, militarily.

We had unquestionably seriously interfered with their government, and we had prevented them from conquering us. That was the sum of our achievement.

We had reached in July last the high-water mark of what we could do in the way of economic and military resistance.

The British had a bad case. World sympathy was not with them. They had been oppressing us with murderous violence. At the same time they preached elsewhere the new world doctrine of "government by consent of the governed". They, too, had reached their high-water mark. They had the power, the force, the armament, to re-conquer us, but they hesitated to exercise that power without getting a world mandate. But, though they had failed in their present attempt, their troops were still in possession of our island. At the time of the Truce they were, in fact, drafting additional and huge levies into Ireland.

We had recognised our inability to beat the British out of Ireland, and we recognised what that inability meant. Writing in the weekly called "The Republic of Ireland" on 21st February last, Mr. Barton, a former member of the *Dáil* Cabinet, stated, that, before the Truce of July 11th it "had become plain that it was physically impossible to secure Ireland's ideal of a completely isolated Republic otherwise than by driving the overwhelmingly superior British forces out of the country".

We also recognised facts in regard to North-East Ulster. We clearly recognised that our national view was not shared by the majority in the four north-eastern counties. We knew that the majority had refused to give allegiance to an Irish Republic.

Before we entered the Conference we realised these facts among ourselves. We had abandoned, for the time being, the hope of achieving the ideal of independence under the Republican form.

It is clear, that the British on their side knew that unless we obtained a real, substantial freedom we would resist to the end at no matter what cost. But they also knew that they could make a "generous" settlement with us. They knew equally well that an offer of such a settlement would disarm the world criticism which could no longer be ignored. They knew they could do these two major things and still preserve the "nations of the British Commonwealth" from violent disruption.

The British believed (and still believe) that they need not, and could not, acquiesce in secession by us, that they need not, and could not, acquiesce in the establishment of a Republican government so close to their own shores. This would be regarded by them as a challenge—a defiance which would be a danger to the very safety of England herself. It would be presented in this light to the people of England. It would be represented as a disruption of the British Empire and would form a headline for other places. South Africa would be the first to follow our example and Britain's security and prestige would be gone. The British spokesmen believed they dared not agree to such a forcible breaking away. It would show not only their Empire to be intolerable, but themselves feeble and futile.

Looking forward through the operation of world forces to the development of freedom, it is certain that at some time acquiescence in the ultimate separation of the units will come. The American colonies of Britain got their freedom by a successful war. Canada, South Africa, and the other States of the British Commonwealth are approaching the same end by peaceful growth. In this Britain acquiesces. Separation by peaceful stages of evolution does not expose her and does not endanger her.

In judging the merits, in examining the details, of the peace we brought back these factors must be taken into consideration.

Before accepting the invitation sent by Mr. Lloyd George, on behalf of his Cabinet, to a Conference, we endeavoured to get an unfettered basis for that Conference. We did not succeed. It is true we reasserted our claim that our Plenipotentiaries could only enter such a Conference as the spokesmen of an independent Sovereign State. It is equally true that this claim

was tacitly admitted by Britain in inviting us to negotiate at all, but the final phase was that we accepted
the invitation "to ascertain how the association of Ireland with the group of nations known as the British
Commonwealth may best be reconciled with Irish
national aspirations".

The invitation opened up the questions, What is the
position of the nations forming the British Commonwealth, and how could our national aspirations best be
reconciled with associations with those nations?
Legally and obsoletely the nations of the Commonwealth are in a position of subservience to Britain.
Constitutionally they occupy to-day a position of freedom and of equality with their mother country.

Sir Robert Borden, in the Peace Treaty debate in the
Canadian House on September 2nd, 1919, claimed for
Canada a "complete sovereignty". This claim has never
been challenged by Britain. It has, in fact, been allowed
by Mr. Bonar Law. General Smuts, in a debate on the
same subject in the Union House on September 10th,
1919, said: "We have secured a position of absolute
equality and freedom, not only among the other States of
the Empire, but among the other nations of the world."

In other words, the former dependent Dominions
of the British Commonwealth are now free and secure
in their freedom.

That position of freedom, and of freedom from
interference, we have secured in the Treaty. The Irish
Plenipotentiaries forced from the British Plenipotentiaries the admission that our status in association
with the British nations would be the constitutional
status of Canada.

The definition of that status is the bedrock of the Treaty. It is the recognition of our right to freedom, and a freedom which shall not be challenged.

No arrangements afterwards mentioned in the Treaty, mutual arrangements agreed upon between our nation and the British nation, can interfere with or derogate from the position which the mention of that status gives us.

The Treaty is but the expression of the terms upon which the British were willing to evacuate—the written recognition of the freedom which such evacuation in itself secures.

We got in the Treaty the strongest guarantees of freedom and security that we could have got on paper, the strongest guarantees that we could have got in a Treaty between Great Britain and ourselves. The most realistic demonstration of the amount of real practical freedom acquired was the evacuation of the British troops and the demobilisation of the military police force. In place of the British troops we have our own army. In place of the Royal Irish Constabulary we are organising our own Civic Guard—our own People's Police Force.

These things are the things of substance; these things are the safe and genuine proof that the status secured by the Treaty is what we claim it to be. They are the plainest definition of our independence; they are the clearest recognition of our national rights. They give us the surest power to maintain both our independence and rights.

It is the evacuation by the British which gives us our freedom. The Treaty is the guarantee that that freedom shall not be violated. The States of the British Commonwealth have the advantage over us of distance. They have the security which that distance gives. They have their freedom. Whatever their nominal position in relation to Britain may be, they can maintain their freedom aided by their distance.

We have not the advantage of distance. Our nearness would be a disadvantage to us under whatever form, and in whatever circumstances, we had obtained our freedom (in case of a feeling of hostility between the two countries, the nearness is, of course, more than a disadvantage to us—it is a standing danger). It was the task of the Plenipotentiaries to overcome this geographical condition in so far as any written arrangement could overcome it.

We succeeded in securing a written recognition of our status. The Treaty clauses covering this constitute a pledge that we shall be as safe from interference as Canada is safe owing to the fact of her four thousand miles of geographical separation.

Our immunity can never be challenged without challenging the immunity of Canada. Having the same constitutional status as Canada, a violation of our freedom would be a challenge to the freedom of Canada. It gives a security which we ought not lightly to despise. No such security would have been reached by the external association aimed at in Document No. 2.

The Treaty is the signed agreement between Britain and ourselves. It is the recognition of our freedom by Britain, and it is the assurance that, having withdrawn her troops, Britain will not again attempt to interfere with that freedom. The free nations of the

Commonwealth are witnesses to Britain's signature. The occupation of our ports for defensive purposes might appear to be a challenge to our security. It is not. The naval facilities are *granted* by us to Britain, and are *accepted* by her in the Treaty as by one independent nation from another by international agreement. For any purpose of interference with us these facilities cannot be used.

At the best, these facilities are, the British say, necessary for the protection of the arteries of their economic and commercial life. At the worst, they are but the expression of the fact that we are at present militarily weaker. Negotiations, therefore treaties, are the expressions of adjustments, of agreements, between two nations as to the terms on which one side will acquiesce in the proposals of the other.

The arrangement provided in the Treaty in regard to North-East Ulster is also but a matter of agreement between ourselves and Britain. It is an agreement by us that we will deal with the difficulty created by Britain. It is an assurance that we will give the North-East certain facilities to enable them to take their place willingly in the Irish Nation.

The maligned Treaty Oath was a further admission wrung from Britain of the real relationship between the British nations. Canada and South Africa continue to swear allegiance to King George, his heirs, successors, etc. They give an oath in keeping with their obsolete position of independence, but out of keeping with their actual position of freedom. Mr. de Valera's alternative oath recognised the King of England as head of the Association—a head inferring subordinates. The

Treaty Oath, however, expresses faithfulness only as symbolical of that association, and is, therefore, really a declaration that each party will be faithful to the compact.

The Irish Plenipotentiaries have been described as "incompetent amateurs". They were, it is said, cajoled and tricked by the wily and experienced British Prime Minister. By means of the fight we put up in the war, by means of the fight we put up in the negotiations, we got the British to evacuate our country. Not only to evacuate it militarily, but to evacuate it socially and economically as well. In addition, we got from the British a signed undertaking to respect the freedom which these evacuations give us.

We acquiesced, in return, to be associated with the British Commonwealth of Nations for certain international purposes. We granted to Britain certain naval facilities.

There is the bargain. It is for the Irish and for our friends the world over to judge whether the "incompetent amateurs" who formed the Irish delegation of Plenipotentiaries forgot their country in making it. If our national aspirations could only have been expressed by the full Republican ideal, then they were not, and never could be, reconciled with what was understood by "association with the group of nations known as the British Empire".

By accepting that invitation we agreed, however some may now deceive themselves and attempt to deceive others, that we would acquiesce in some association. In return for that acquiescence we expected something tangible—evacuation, abandonment of

British aggression. If we had been martially victorious over Britain there would have been no question of such acquiescence.

Now, if that is so, and it is so, the surrender of some national sentiment was for the time unavoidable. The British Empire, the British Commonwealth, or the British League of Free Nations—it does not matter what name you call it—is what it is. It is what it is, with all its trappings of feudalism, its symbols of monarchy, its feudal phraseology, its obsolete oaths of allegiance, its King a figurehead having no individual power as King, maintaining the unhealthy atmosphere of mediaeval subservience translated into modern snobbery. All this is doubly offensive to us, offensive to our Gaelic instincts of social equality which recognises only an aristocracy of the mind, and offensive from the memories of hundreds of years of tyranny carried out in the name of the British King.

Those who could not, or who would not, look these facts in the face blame us now, and more than blame us. They find fault with us that, in agreeing to some kind of association of our nation with the British nations, we were not able, by the touch of a magic wand, to get rid of all the language of Empire. That is not a fair attitude. We like that language no more, perhaps less, than do those who wish to make us responsible for its preservation. It is Britain's affair, not ours, that she cares to preserve these prevarications.

Let us look to what we have undoubtedly gained and not to what we might have gained. Let us see how the maximum value can be realised from that gain. If we would only put away dreams, and face realities, nearly all the things that count we have now for our country.

What we want is that Ireland shall be Ireland in spirit as well as in name. It is not any verbiage about sovereignty which can assure our power to shape our destinies. It is to grasp everything which is of benefit to us, to manage these things for ourselves, to get rid of the unIrish atmosphere and influence, to make our government and restore our national life on the lines which suit our national character and our national requirements best. It is now only fratricidal strife which can prevent us from making the Gaelic Ireland which is our goal.

The test of the Government we want is whether it conforms with Irish tradition and national character? Whether it will suit us and enable us to live socially and prosper? Whether we can achieve something which our old free Irish democratic life would have developed into?

We have shaken off the foreign domination which prevented us from living our own life in our own way. We are now free to do this. It depends on ourselves alone whether we can do it.

DISTINCTIVE CULTURE
Ancient Irish Civilization
Glories of the Past

I t was not only by the British armed occupation
that Ireland was subdued. It was by means of the
destruction, after great effort, of our Gaelic civilization. This destruction brought upon us the loss
almost of nationality itself. For the last 100 years or
more Ireland has been a nation in little more than in
name.

Britain wanted us for her own economic ends, as
well as to satisfy her love of conquest. It was found,
however, that Ireland was not an easy country to con-
quer, nor to use for the purposes for which conquests
are made. We had a native culture. We had a social
system of our own. We had an economic organisation.
We had a code of laws which fitted us.

These were such in their beauty, their honesty,
their recognition of right and justice, and in their
strength, that foreigners coming to our island brought
with them nothing of like attractiveness to replace
them. These foreigners accepted Irish civilization,
forgot their own, and eagerly became absorbed into
the Irish race.

Ireland, unlike Britain, had never become a part of the Roman Empire. Even if the Romans had invaded Ireland, and had been able to get a foothold, it is not probable that they would have succeeded in imposing their form of government. At that time our native civilization had become well advanced. It had advanced far past the primitive social state of the Britons and of other of the North European peoples.

And it had, through its democratic basis, which would have been strengthened and adapted as time went on, a health and permanence which would have enabled it to withstand the rivalry of the autocratic government of Rome, which always had in it the seeds of decay.

The Romans invaded Britain and imposed their government till it was destroyed by fresh invaders. And the history of England, unlike the history of Ireland, was one in which each new invasion altered the social polity of the people. Foreigners were not absorbed as in Ireland. England was affected by every fresh incursion, and English civilization to-day is the reflection of such changes.

The Roman armies did not come to Ireland. But Ireland was known to the merchants of the Empire, who brought with them not only commerce but art and culture. Ireland took from them what was of advantage, and our civilization went on growing in strength and harmony. It grew more and more to fit the Irish people, and became the expression of them. It could never have been destroyed except by deliberate uprooting aided by military violence.

The Irish social and economic system was democratic. It was simple and harmonious. The people had security in their rights, and just law. And, suited to them, their economic life progressed smoothly. Our people had leisure for the things in which they took delight. They had leisure for the cultivation of the mind, by the study of art, literature, and the traditions. They developed character and bodily strength by acquiring skill in military exercise and in the national games.

The pertinacity of Irish civilization was due to the democratic basis of its economic system, and the aristocracy of its culture.

It was the reverse of Roman civilization in which the State was held together by a central authority, controlling and defending it, the people being left to themselves in all social and intellectual matters. Highly organised, Roman civilization was powerful, especially for subduing and dominating other races, for a time. But not being rooted in the interests and respect of the people themselves, it could not survive.

Gaelic civilization was quite different. The people of the whole nation were united, not by material forces, but by spiritual ones. Their unity was not of any military solidarity. It came from sharing the same traditions. It came from honouring the same heroes, from inheriting the same literature, from willing obedience to the same law, the law which was their own law and reverenced by them.

They never exalted a central authority. Economically they were divided up into a number of larger and smaller units. Spiritually and socially they were one people.

Each community was independent and complete within its own boundaries. The land belonged to the people. It was held for the people by the Chief of the Clan. He was their trustee. He secured his position by the will of the people only. His successor was elected by the people.

The privileges and duties of the chiefs, doctors, lawyers, bards, were the same throughout the country. The schools were linked together in a national system. The bards and historians travelled from one community to another. The schools for the study of law, medicine, history, military skill, belonged to the whole nation, and were frequented by those who were chosen by each community to be their scholars.

The love of learning and of military skill was the tradition of the whole people. They honoured not kings nor chiefs as kings and chiefs, but their heroes and their great men. Their men of high learning ranked with the kings and sat beside them in equality at the high table.

It was customary for all the people to assemble together on fixed occasions to hear the law expounded and the old heroic tales recited. The people themselves contributed. They competed with each other in the games. These assemblies were the expression of our Irish civilization and one of the means by which it was preserved.

Thus Ireland was a country made up of a large number of economically independent units. But in the things of the mind and spirit the nation was one.

This democratic social polity, with the exaltation of the things of the mind and character, are the essence of ancient Irish civilization, and must provide the keynote for the new.

It suited our character and genius. While we were able to preserve it no outside enemy had any power against us. While it survived our subjection was impossible. But our invaders learned its strength and set out to destroy it.

English civilization, while it may suit the English people, could only be alien to us. It is English civilization, fashioned out of their history. For us it is a misfit. It is a garment, not something within us. We are mean, clumsy, and ungraceful, wearing it. It exposes all our defects while giving us no scope to display our good qualities. Our external and internal life has become the expression of its unfitness. The Gaelic soul of the Irish people still lives. In itself it is indestructible. But its qualities are hidden, besmirched, by that which has been imposed upon us, just as the fine, splendid surface of Ireland is besmirched by our towns and villages—hideous medleys of contemptible dwellings and mean shops and squalid public-houses, not as they should be in material fitness, the beautiful human expressions of what our God-given country is.

It is only in the remote corners of Ireland in the South and West and North-West that any trace of the old Irish civilization is met with now. To those places the social side of anglicisation was never able very easily to penetrate. To-day it is only in those places that any native beauty and grace in Irish life survive. And these are the poorest parts of our country!

In the island of Achill, impoverished as the people are, hard as their lives are, difficult as the struggle for existence is, the outward aspect is a pageant. One may see processions of young women riding down on the island ponies to collect sand from the seashore, or gathering in the turf, dressed in their shawls and in their brilliantly-coloured skirts made of material spun, woven, and dyed, by themselves, as it has been spun, woven, and dyed, for over a thousand years. Their cottages also are little changed. They remain simple and picturesque. It is only in such places that one gets a glimpse of what Ireland may become again, when the beauty may be something more than a pageant, will be the outward sign of a prosperous and happy Gaelic life.

Our internal life too has become the expression of the misfit of English civilization. With all their natural intelligence, the horizon of many of our people has become bounded by the daily newspaper, the public-house, and the racecourse. English civilization made us into the stage Irishman, hardly a caricature.

They destroyed our language, all but destroyed it, and in giving us their own they cursed us so that we have become its slaves. Its words seem with us almost an end in themselves, and not as they should be, the medium for expressing our thoughts.

We have now won the first victory. We have secured the departure of the enemy who imposed upon us that by which we were debased, and by means of which he kept us in subjection. We only succeeded after we had begun to get back our Irish ways, after we had made a serious effort to speak our own language, after we had striven again to govern ourselves. We can only keep out the enemy, and all other enemies, by completing that task.

We are now free in name. The extent to which we become free in fact and secure our freedom will be the extent to which we become Gaels again. It is a hard task. The machine of the British armed force, which tried to crush us, we could see with our physical eyes. We could touch it. We could put our physical strength against it. We could see their agents in uniform and under arms. We could see their tanks and armoured cars.

But the spiritual machine which has been mutilating us, destroying our customs, and our independent life, is not so easy to discern. We have to seek it out with the eyes of our mind. We have to put against it the whole weight of our united spiritual strength. And it has become so familiar, how are we to recognise it?

We cannot, perhaps. But we can do something else. We can replace it. We can fill our minds with Gaelic ideas, and our lives with Gaelic customs, until there is no room for any other.

It is not any international association of our nation with the British nations which is going to hinder us in that task. It lies in our own hands. Upon us will rest the praise or blame of the real freedom we make for ourselves or the absence of it.

The survival of some connection with our former enemy, since it has no power to chain us, should act as a useful irritant. It should be a continual reminder of how near we came to being, indeed, a British nation. No one now has any power to make us that but ourselves alone.

We have to build up a new civilization on the foundations of the old. And it is not the leaders of the Irish people who can do it for the people. They can but point the way. They can but do their best to establish a reign of justice and of law and order which will enable the people to do it for themselves.

It is not to political leaders our people must look, but to themselves. Leaders are but individuals, and individuals are imperfect, liable to error and weakness. The strength of the nation will be the strength of the spirit of the whole people. We must have a political, economic, and social system in accordance with our national character.

It must be a system in which our material, intellectual, and spiritual needs and tastes will find expression and satisfaction. We shall then grow to be in ourselves and in what we produce, and in the villages, towns, and cities in which we live, and in our homes, an expression of the light which is within us, as now we are in nearly all those things an indication of the darkness which has enveloped us for so long.

Economically we must be democratic, as in the past. The right of all the people must be secure. The people must become again "the guardians of their law and of their land". Each must be free to reap the full reward of his labour. Monopoly must not be allowed to deprive anyone of that right.

Neither, through the existence of monopoly, must capital be allowed to be an evil. It must not be allowed to draw away all the fruits of labour to itself. It must fulfil its proper function of being the means by which are brought forth fresh and fuller fruits for the benefit of all.

With real democracy in our economic life, country districts would become again living centres. The people would again be co-operating in industry, and co-operating and competing in pleasure and in culture. Our countrysides would cease to be the torpid deserts they are now, giving the means of existence and nothing more.

Our Government must be democratic in more than in name. It must be the expression of the people's wishes. It must carry out for them all, and only, what is needed to be done for the people as a whole. It must not interfere with what the people can do for themselves in their own centres. We must not have State Departments headed by a politician whose only qualification is that he has climbed to a certain rung in the political ladder.

The biggest task will be the restoration of the language. How can we express our most subtle thoughts and finest feelings in a foreign tongue? Irish will scarcely be our language in this generation, not even perhaps in the next. But until we have it again on our tongues and in our minds we are not free, and we will produce no immortal literature.

Our music and our art and literature must be in the lives of the people themselves, not as in England, the luxury of the few. England has produced some historians, many great poets, and a few great artists, but they are the treasures of the cultured minority and have no place in the lives of the main body of the English people.

Our poets and artists will be inspired in the stimulating air of freedom to be something more than the mere producers of verse and painters of pictures. They will teach us, by their vision, the noble race we may become, expressed in their poetry and their pictures. They will inspire us to live as Irish men and Irish women should. They have to show us the way, and the people will then in their turn become the inspiration of the poets and artists of the future Gaelic Ireland.

Our civilization will be glorious or the reverse, according to the character of the people. And the work we produce will be the expression of what we are. Our external life has become the expression of all we have been deprived of—something shapeless, ugly, without native life. But the spark of native life is still there and can be fanned into flame.

What we have before us is the great work of building up our nation. No soft road—a hard road, but inspiring and exalting. Irish art and Irish customs must be revived, and must be carried out by the people themselves, helped by a central Government, not controlled and managed by it; helped by departments of music, art, national painting, etc., with local centres connected with them.

The commercialising of these things—art, literature, music, the drama—as is done in other countries, must be discouraged. Everybody being able to contribute, we would have a skilled audience, criticising and appreciating, and not only, as in England, paying for seats to hear famous performers, but for real appreciative enjoyment and education.

Our national education must provide a balance of the competing elements—the real education of the faculties, and storing the mind with the best thoughts of the great men of our own and other nations. And there must be education by special training for trades and professions for the purpose of scientific eminence in medicine, law, agriculture, and commerce. And, as fit habitations for healthy minds, we must have healthy bodies. We shall have these by becoming again skilled in military prowess and skilled in our Gaelic games, which develop strength and nerve and muscle. They teach us resource, courage, and co-operation. These games provide for our civil life those qualities of ingenuity and daring which military training teaches for the purposes of war.

Our army, if it exists for honourable purposes only, will draw to it honourable men. It will call to it the best men of our race—men of skill and culture. It will not be recruited as so many modern armies are, from those who are industrially useless.

This will certainly be so, for our army will only exist for the defence of our liberties, and of our people in the exercise of their liberties. An Irish army can never be used for the ignoble purpose of invasion, subjugation, and exploitation.

But it is not only upon our army that our security will depend. It will depend more upon the extent to which we make ourselves invulnerable by having a civilization which is indestructible. That civilization will only be indestructible by being enthroned in the lives of the people, and having its foundation resting on right, honesty, and justice.

Our army will be but secondary in maintaining our security. Its strength will be but the strength of real resistance—the extent to which we build up within ourselves what can never be invaded and what can never be destroyed—the extent to which we make strong the spirit of the Irish Nation.

We are a small nation. Our military strength in proportion to the mighty armaments of modern nations can never be considerable. Our strength as a nation will depend upon our economic freedom, and upon our moral and intellectual force. In these we can become a shining light in the world.

BUILDING UP IRELAND
Resources to be Developed

M r. de Valera, in a speech he made on February 19, warned the people of Ireland against a life of ease, against living practically "the life of the beasts", which, he fears, they may be tempted to do in Ireland under the Free State.

The chance that materialism will take possession of the Irish people is no more likely in a free Ireland under the Free State than it would be in a free Ireland under a Republican or any other form of government. It is in the hands of the Irish people themselves.

In the ancient days of Gaelic civilization the people were prosperous and they were not materialists. They were one of the most spiritual and one of the most intellectual peoples in Europe. When Ireland was swept by destitution and famine the spirit of the Irish people came most nearly to extinction. It was with the improved economic conditions of the last twenty years or more that it has re-awakened. The insistent needs of the body more adequately satisfied, the people regained desire once more to reach out to the higher things in which the spirit finds its satisfaction.

What we hope for in the new Ireland is to have such material welfare as will give the Irish spirit that freedom. We want such widely diffused prosperity that the Irish people will not be crushed by destitution into living practically "the lives of the beasts". They were so crushed during the British occupation that they were described as being "without the comforts of an English sow". Neither must they be obliged, owing to unsound economic conditions, to spend all their powers of both mind and body in an effort to satisfy the bodily needs alone. The uses of wealth are to provide good health, comfort, moderate luxury, and to give the freedom which comes from the possession of these things.

Our object in building up the country economically must not be lost sight of. That object is not to be able to boast of enormous wealth or of a great volume of trade, for their own sake. It is not to see our country covered with smoking chimneys and factories. It is not to show a great national balance-sheet, nor to point to a people producing wealth with the self-obliteration of a hive of bees.

The real riches of the Irish nation will be the men and women of the Irish nation, the extent to which they are rich in body and mind and character.

What we want is the opportunity for everyone to be able to produce sufficient wealth to ensure these advantages for themselves. That such wealth can be produced in Ireland there can be no doubt: "For the island is so endowed with so many dowries of nature, considering the fruitfulness of the soil, the ports, the rivers, the fishings, and especially the race and generation of men, valiant, hard, and active, as it is not easy to find such a confluence of commodities." Such was the impression made upon a visitor who came long ago to our island. We have now the opportunities to make our land indeed fruitful, to work up our natural resources, to bring prosperity for all our people.

If our national economy is put on a sound footing from the beginning it will, in the new Ireland, be possible for our people to provide themselves with the ordinary requirements of decent living. It will be possible for each to have sufficient food, a good home in which to live in fair comfort and contentment. We shall be able to give our children bodily and mental health; and our people will be able to secure themselves against the inevitable times of sickness and old age.

That must be our object. What we must aim at is the building up of a sound economic life in which great discrepancies cannot occur. We must not have the destitution of poverty at one end, and at the other an excess of riches in the possession of a few individuals, beyond what they can spend with satisfaction and justification.

Millionaires can spend their surplus wealth bestowing libraries broadcast upon the world. But who will say that the benefits accruing could compare with those arising from a condition of things in which the people themselves everywhere, in the city, town, and village, were prosperous enough to buy their own books and to put together their own local libraries in which they could take a personal interest and acquire knowledge in proportion to that interest?

The growing wealth of Ireland will, we hope, be diffused through all our people, all sharing in the growing prosperity, each receiving according to what each contributes in the making of that prosperity, so that the weal of all is assured.

How are we to increase the wealth of Ireland and ensure that all producing it shall share in it? That is the question which will be engaging the minds of our people, and will engage the attention of the new Government.

The keynote to the economic revival must be development of Irish resources by Irish capital for the benefit of the Irish consumer in such a way that the people have steady work at just remuneration and their own share of control.

How are we to develop Irish resources? The earth is our bountiful mother. Upon free access to it depends not only agriculture, but all other trades and industries. Land must be freely available. Agriculture, our main industry, must be improved and developed. Our existing industries must be given opportunities to expand. Conditions must be created which will make it possible for new ones to arise. Means of transit must be extended and cheapened. Our harbours must be developed. Our water-power must be utilised; our mineral resources must be exploited.

Foreign trade must be stimulated by making facilities for the transport and marketing of Irish goods abroad and foreign goods in Ireland. Investors must be urged and encouraged to invest Irish capital in

Irish concerns. Taxation, where it hinders, must be adjusted, and must be imposed where the burden will fall lightest and can best be borne, and where it will encourage rather than discourage industry.

We have now in Ireland, owing to the restrictions put upon emigration during the European war, a larger population of young men and women than we have had for a great many years. For their own sake and to maintain the strength of the nation room must and can be found for them.

Agriculture is, and is likely to continue to be, our chief source of wealth. If room is to be found for our growing population, land must be freely available. Land is not freely available in Ireland. Thousands of acres of the best land lie idle or are occupied as ranches or form part of extensive private estates.

Side by side with this condition there are thousands of our people who are unable to get land on which to keep a cow or even to provide themselves and their families with vegetables.

If the ranches can be broken up, if we can get the land back again into the hands of our people, there will be plenty of employment and a great increase in the national wealth.

If land could be obtained more cheaply in town and country the housing problem would not present so acute a problem. There are large areas unoccupied in towns and cities as well as in country districts. When the Convention sat in 1917 it was found that in urban areas alone, 67,000 houses were urgently needed. The figure must at the present moment be considerably higher. To ease the immediate situation, the Provisional Government has announced a grant to enable a considerable number of houses to be built. This grant, although seemingly large, is simply a recognition of the existence of the problem.

For those who intend to engage in agriculture we require specialised education. Agriculture is in these days a highly technical industry. We have the experiences of countries like Holland, Germany, Denmark to guide us. Scientific methods of farming and stock-raising must be introduced. We must have the study of specialised chemistry to aid us, as it does our foreign competitors in the countries I have named. We must establish industries arising directly out of agriculture, industries for the utilisation of the by-products of the land—bones, bristles, hides for the production of soda glue, and other valuable substances.

With plenty of land available at an economic rent or price such industries can be established throughout the country districts, opening up new opportunities for employment.

Up to the sixteenth century Ireland possessed a colonial trade equal to England's. It was destroyed by the jealousy of English ship-owners and manufacturers, and, by means of the Navigation Laws, England swept Ireland's commerce off the seas. It is true that these Navigation Laws were afterwards removed. But the removal found the Irish capital which might have restored our ruined commerce drained away from the country by the absence of opportunities for utilising it, or by absentee landlordism, or in other ways.

The development of industry in the new Ireland should be on lines which exclude monopoly profits. The product of industry would thus be left sufficiently free to supply good wages to those employed in it. The system should be on co-operative lines rather than on the old commercial capitalistic lines of the huge joint stock companies. At the same time I think we shall safely avoid State Socialism, which has nothing to commend it in a country like Ireland, and, in any case, is monopoly of another kind.

Given favourable conditions, there is a successful future for dressed meat industries on the lines of the huge co-operative industry started in Wexford; while there are many opportunities for the extension of dairying and cheese-making.

The industries we possess are nearly all capable of expansion. We can improve and extend all the following:

> Brewing and distilling.
> Manufacture of tobacco.
> Woollen and linen industry.
> Manufacture of hosiery and underclothing.
> Rope and twine industry.
> Manufacture of boots and shoes, saddlery, and all kinds of leather articles.
> Production of hardware and agricultural machinery.
> Production and curing of fish.

Of manufactured articles £48,000,000 worth are imported into Ireland yearly. A large part of these could be produced more economically at home. If land were procurable abundantly and cheaply it would be necessary also that capital should be forthcoming to get suitable sites for factories, a more easily obtained supply of power, an improvement, increase, and cheapening of the means of transport. There are facilities for producing an enormous variety of products both for the home and foreign markets, if factories could be established. These should, as far as possible, be dispersed about the country instead of being concentrated in a few areas. This disposal will not only have the effect of avoiding congestion, but will incidentally improve the status and earnings of the country population and will enlarge their horizon.

I am not advocating the establishment of an industrial system as other countries know industrialism. If we are to survive as a distinct and free nation, industrial development must be on the general lines I am following. Whatever our solution of the question may be, we all realise that the industrial *status quo* is imperfect. However we may differ in outlook, politically or socially, it is recognised that one of the most pressing needs—if not the most pressing—is the question of labour in relation to industry, and it is consequently vitally necessary for the development of our resources that the position of employers and employees should rest on the best possible foundation.

And with this question of labour and industry is interwoven the question of land. It is no less important to have our foundations secure here. In the development of Ireland the land question presents itself under four main headings:

(1) The completion of purchase of tenanted lands;

(2) The extension and increase of powers of purchase of untenanted lands;

(3) The question of congestion in rural districts:

(4) The utilisation of lands unoccupied or withheld in urban areas.

For the purpose of such development Ireland has three great natural resources. Our coal deposits are by no means inconsiderable. The bogs of Ireland are estimated as having 500,000 million tons of peat fuel. Water-power is concentrated in her 237 rivers and 180 lakes. The huge Lough Corrib system could be utilised, for instance, to work the granite in the neighbourhood of Galway. In the opinion of experts, reporting to the Committee on the Water-Power Resources of Ireland, from the Irish lakes and rivers a total of 500,000 h.p. is capable of being developed.

The magnitude of this is more readily seen if it is appreciated that to raise this power in steam would require 7,500,000 tons of coal. With the present price of coal it should be a commercial proposition to develop our water-power as against steam, even though it did not take the place of steam-power entirely.

Schemes have been worked out to utilise the water-power of the Shannon, the Erne, the Bann, and the Liffey. It is probable that the Liffey and the Bann, being closely connected with industrial centres, can be dealt with at once. With unified control and direction, various sources of water-power could be arranged in large stations for centralised industries, and the energy could be redistributed to provide light and heat for the neighbouring towns and villages.

That the advantages of our water-power are not lost on some of the keenest minds of the day is shown by the following extract from a speech made by Lord Northcliffe on St. Patrick's Day, 1917: "The growth of the population of Great Britain has been largely due to manufactures based on the great asset, black coal. Ireland has none of the coal which has made England rich, but she possesses in her mighty rivers white coal of which millions of horse-power are being lost to Ireland every year...I can see in the future very plainly prosperous cities, old and new, fed by the greatest river in the United Kingdom—the Shannon. I should like to read recent experts' reports on the Moy, the Suir, and the Lee."

The development of this white power will also enable the means of communication and transport by rail and road to be cheapened and extended. And there is an urgent need for cheap transit. Railway rates and shipping rates are so high that, to take one example, the cost of transit is prohibitive to the Irish fish trade.

While the Irish seas are teeming with fish, we have the Dublin market depending upon the English market for its supplies. The export of Irish fish is decreasing, and the fishing industry is neither the source of remuneration it should be to those engaged in it, nor the source of profit it could be to the country.

To facilitate the transport of agricultural produce and commodities generally, a complete system of ways of communication must be established. The extension and unifying of our railways, linking up ocean ports and fishing harbours with the interior, is essential. This system will be worked in connection with our inland waterways, and will be supplemented by a motor-lorry service on our roads—and these also must be greatly improved.

Our harbours must be developed. Ireland occupies a unique geographical position. She is the stepping-stone between the Old World and the New. She should therefore, become a great exchange mart between Europe and America. With Galway harbour improved and developed so as to receive American liners, passengers could land in Europe one or two days earlier than by disembarking at Liverpool.

The port and docks of Dublin are already making arrangements for a great increase in the volume of trade which is expected with the establishment of an Irish Government in Dublin. They are improving the port. They have schemes for providing deep water berthage for the largest ships afloat.

Soon the port of Dublin will be fitted in every way to receive and deal with all the trade which may be expected with our growing prosperity. The Board is also reclaiming land at the mouth of the Liffey, and soon some sixty acres will be available as a building site. This land is splendidly situated for commercial purposes.

It will be important to create efficient machinery for the economic marketing of Irish goods. A first step in this direction is the establishment of a clearing house in Dublin or the most convenient centre. It would form a link between a network of channels throughout Ireland through which goods could be transmitted, connecting with another network reaching out to all our markets abroad. It would examine and take delivery of goods going out and coming in, dealing with the financial business for both sides.

Such a concern would require capital and able and experienced management. With such, its success should be assured. It would be invaluable in helping our home and foreign trade. And with improved means of transit in Ireland, and an increase in the number of direct shipping routes, facilities would be in existence to make it operate successfully. It is not difficult to see the advantages of such a house. On the one hand it would be closely associated in location and business working with a central railway station where the important trunk lines converged, and on the other conveniently situated in relation to the National Customs House.

The mineral resources of Ireland have never been properly tapped. An Irish Government will not neglect this important source of wealth. The development of mines and minerals will be on national lines, and under national direction. This will prevent the monopoly by private individuals of what are purely national resources belonging to all the people of the nation. The profits from all these national enterprises—the working of mines, development of waterpower, etc.—will belong to the nation for the advantage of the whole nation.

But Irish men and women as private individuals must do their share to increase the prosperity of the country. Business cannot succeed without capital. Millions of Irish money are lying idle in banks. The deposits in Irish joint stock banks increased in the aggregate by £7,318,000 during the half-year ended December 31, 1921. At that date the total of deposits and cash balances in the Irish banks was £194,391,000, to which in addition there was a sum of almost £14,000,000 in the Post Office Savings Bank. If Irish money were invested in Irish industries, to assist existing ones, and to finance new enterprises, there would be an enormous development of Irish commerce.

The Irish people have a large amount of capital invested abroad. With scope for our energies, with restoration of confidence, the inevitable tendency will be towards return of this capital to Ireland. It will then flow in its proper channel. It will be used for opening up new and promising fields in this country. Ireland will provide splendid opportunities for the investment of Irish capital, and it is for the Irish people to take advantage of these opportunities.

If they do not, investors and exploiters from outside will come in to reap the rich profits which are to be made. And, what is worse still, they will bring with them all the evils that we want to avoid in the new Ireland.

We shall hope to see in Ireland industrial conciliation and arbitration taking the place of strikes, and the workers sharing in the ownership and management of businesses.

A prosperous Ireland will mean a united Ireland. With equitable taxation and flourishing trade our North-East countrymen will need no persuasion to come in and share in the healthy economic life of the country.

FREEDOM WITHIN OUR GRASP

For Ourselves to Achieve It

Work of Gaelic League and Sinn Féin

The freedom which has been won is the fruit of the national efforts of this generation and of preceding ones, and to judge the merits of that fruit it is necessary to recall those efforts. It is necessary to look back, and to see each one arising out of each loss which the nation sustained.

We see them working along their separate but converging lines—some mere trickling streams, others broad tributaries, but all which had sufficient strength and right direction reaching, becoming merged in, and swelling the volume of the river which flows on to freedom.

Up to the Union English interference in Ireland had succeeded only in its military and economic oppression. The national spirit survived. The country had been disarmed after the Treaty of Limerick. The land of Ireland had been confiscated. Native industry and commerce were attacked and had been crippled or destroyed, but Gaelic nationality lived on. The people spoke their own language, preserved their Gaelic customs and ways of life, and remained united in their common traditions. They had no inducement to look outside their own country, and entrenched behind their language and their national traditions, they kept their social life intact. Ireland was still the Ireland of the wholly distinctive Irish people.

The efforts of resistance made by the nation were the expressions of what had been robbed from the nation. There were military uprisings to resist some new oppression, but these were also the unconscious protests of a nation's right to defend itself by force of arms. There were also peaceful attempts to recover economic, or political, or religious freedom through the Parliament in Dublin.

With the Union came upheaval. The scene of government was transferred to England. The garrison which was becoming Gaelicised towards the end of the eighteenth century, turned away from Ireland with the destruction of the Dublin Parliament, and made London their Capital.

With Catholic Emancipation and the "right" to have representatives of the Irish people to sit in the foreign parliament, the national spirit was at last invaded. People began to look abroad. The anglicisation of Ireland had begun.

The English language became the language of education and fashion. It penetrated slowly at first. It was aided by the National Schools. In those schools it was the only medium of education for a people who were still Gaelic-speaking.

Side by side with this peaceful penetration, the Irish language decayed, and when the people had adopted a new language and had come to look to England for Government, they learned to see in English customs and English culture the models upon which to fashion their own.

The "gifts" wrung for Ireland (always wrung by agitation more or less violent in Ireland itself, and never as a result of the oratory of the Irish representatives in the British Parliament), Catholic Emancipation, Land Acts, Local Government, where not actually destructive in themselves of the Gaelic social economic system, helped in the denationalisation process.

These things undoubtedly brought ameliorative changes, but the people got into the habit of looking to a foreign authority, and they inevitably came to lose their self-respect, their self-reliance, and their national strength.

The system made them forget to look to themselves, and taught them to turn their backs upon their own country. We became the beggars of the rich neighbours who had robbed us. We lost reverence for our own nation, and we came very near to losing our national identity.

O'Connell was the product of the Ireland which arose out of this perversion. Prompted by the Young Irelanders, and urged on by the zeal of the people, stirred for the moment to national consciousness by the teaching of Davis, he talked of national liberty, but he did nothing to win it. He was a follower and not a leader of the people. He feared any movement of a revolutionary nature. Himself a Gaelic speaker, he adopted the English language, so little did he understand the strength to the nation of its own native language. His aim was little more than to see the Irish people a free Catholic community.

He would have Ireland merely a prosperous province of Britain with no national distinctiveness. Generally speaking, he acquiesced in a situation which was bringing upon the Irish nation spiritual decay.

The Young Irelanders, of whom Thomas Davis was the inspiration, were the real leaders.

They saw and felt more deeply and aimed more truly. Davis spoke to the soul of the sleeping nation—drunk with the waters of forgetfulness. He sought to unite the whole people. He fought against sectarianism and all the other causes which divided them.

He saw that unless we were Gaels we were not a nation. When he thought of the nation he thought of the men and women of the nation. He knew that unless they were free, Ireland could not be free, and to fill them again with pride in their nation he sang to them of the old splendour of Ireland, of their heroes, of their language, of the strength of unity, of the glory of noble strife, of the beauties of the land, of the delights and richness of the Gaelic life.

"A nationality founded in the hearts and intelligence of the people," he said, "would bid defiance to the arms of the foe and guile of the traitor. The first step to nationality is the open and deliberate recognition of it by the people themselves. Once the Irish people declare the disconnection of themselves, their feelings, and interests from the men, feelings, and interests of England, they are in march for freedom."

That was the true National Gospel. "Educate that you may be free," he said. "It was only by baptism at the fount of Gaelicism that we would get the strength and ardour to fit us for freedom."

The spirit of Davis breathed again in those who succeeded to his teaching, and who, directed by that inspiration, kept the footsteps of the nation on the right road for the march to freedom.

The Union was accompanied by both economic and national decay, and the movements of the nineteenth century were the outcome of those two evils.

But one was more a political than a national movement, unconscious of, or indifferent to, the fact that the nation was rapidly dying. Its policy was to concentrate on England and agitate for measures of reform and political emancipation. It was pleading to the spoilers for a portion of the spoils they had robbed from us.

But those who had succeeded to the teachings of Davis saw that if we continued to turn to England the nation would become extinct. We were tacitly accepting England's denial of our nationhood so useful for her propaganda purposes. We were selling our birthright for a mess of pottage.

They saw that the nation could only be preserved and freedom won by the Irish people themselves. We needed to become strong within our nation individually as the self-respecting, self-reliant men and women of the Irish nation; otherwise, we would never get into the "march for freedom".

The new movements were distinct, yet harmonious. They were all built on the same foundation— the necessity for national freedom. They all taught that the people must look to themselves for economic prosperity, and must turn to national culture as a means to national freedom. They reached out to every phase of the people's lives, educating to make them free. No means were too slight to use for that purpose. The Gaelic Athletic Association reminded Irish boys that they were Gaels. It provided and restored national games as an alternative to the slavish adoption of English sport. The Gaelic League restored the language to its place in the reverence of the people. It revived Gaelic culture. While being non-political, it was by its very nature intensely national. Within its folds were nurtured the men and women who were to win for Ireland the power to achieve national freedom. *Irish history will recognise in the birth of the Gaelic League in 1893 the most important event of the nineteenth century.* I may go further and say, not only the nineteenth century, but in the whole history of our nation. It checked the peaceful penetration and once and for all turned the minds of the Irish people back to their own country. It did more than any other movement to restore the national pride, honour, and self-respect. Through the medium of the language it linked the people with the past and led them to look to a future which would be a noble continuation of it.

The *Sinn Féin* movement was both economic and national, meeting, therefore, the two evils produced by the Union. Inspired by Arthur Griffith and William Rooney, it grew to wield enormous educational and spiritual power. It organised the country. It promoted what came to be known as the "Irish-Ireland Policy". It preached the recreation of Ireland built upon the

Gael. It penetrated into Belfast and North-East Ulster, and was doing encouraging educational work, and was making the national revival general when the World War broke out in 1914.

If that work could have been completed, the freedom which has been won would have been completed. Until Ireland can speak to the world with a united distinctive voice, we shall not have earned, and shall not get, that full freedom in all its completeness which nations, that are nations, can never rest until they have achieved.

The *Sinn Féin* movement was not militant, but the militant movement existed within it, and by its side. It had for its advocates the two mightiest figures that have appeared in the whole present movement—Tom Clarke and Seán MacDermott.

The two movements worked in perfect harmony.

Rooney preached language and liberty. He inspired all whom he met with national pride and courage. "Tell the world bravely what we seek," he said. "We must be men if we mean to win." He believed that liberty could not be won unless we were fit and willing to win it, and were ready to suffer and die for it.

He interpreted the national ideal as "an Irish State governed by Irishmen for the benefit of the Irish people". He sought to impregnate the whole people with "a Gaelic-speaking Nationality". "Only then could we win freedom and be worthy of it; freedom—individual and national freedom—of the fullest and broadest character; freedom to think and act as it best beseems; national freedom to stand equally with the rest of the world."

He aimed at weaving Gaelicism into the whole fabric of our national life. He wished to have Gaelic songs sung by the children in the schools. He advocated the boycotting of English goods, always with an eye to the spiritual effect. "We shall need to turn our towns into something more than mere huxters' shops, and as a natural consequence wells of anglicisation poisoning every section of our people."

Only by developing our own resources, by linking up our life with the past, and adopting the civilization which was stopped by the Union could we become Gaels again, and help to win our nation back. As long as we were Gaels, he said, the influence of the foreigner was negligible in Ireland. Unless we were Gaels we had no claim to occupy a definite or distinct place in the world's life.

"We most decidedly do believe that this nation has a right to direct its own destinies. We do most heartily concede that men bred and native of the soil are the best judges of what is good for this land. We are believers in an Irish nation using its own tongue, flying its own flag, defending its own coasts, and using its own discretion when dealing with the outside world. But this we most certainly believe can never come as the gift of any parliament, British or otherwise; it can only be won by the strong right arm and grim resolve of men." "*Neglect no weapon,*" he urged, "*which the necessities and difficulties of the enemy force him to abandon to us, and make each 'concession' a stepping-stone to further things.*"

Rooney spoke as a prophet. He prepared the way and foresaw the victory, and he helped his nation to rise, and, by developing its soul, to get ready for victory.

A good tree brings forth good fruit—a barren one produces nothing. The policy represented by O'Connell, Isaac Butt, and John Redmond ended in impotence.

The freedom which Ireland has achieved was dreamed of by Wolfe Tone, was foreseen by Thomas Davis, and their efforts were broadened out until they took into their embrace all the true national movements by the "grim resolve" of William Rooney, supported later by the "strong right arm" of the Volunteers.

All the streams—economic, political, spiritual, cultural, and militant—met together in the struggle of 1916-21 which has ended in a Peace, in which the Treaty of Limerick is wiped out by the departure of the British armed forces, and the establishment of an Irish Army in their place. In which the Union is wiped out by the establishment of a free native Parliament which will be erected on a Constitution expressing the will of the Irish people.

With the Union came national enslavement. With the termination of the Union goes national enslavement, *if we will*. Freedom from any outside enemy is now ours, and nobody but ourselves can prevent us achieving it.

We are free now to get back and to keep all that was taken from us. We have no choice but to turn our eyes again to Ireland. The most completely anglicised person in Ireland will look to Britain in vain. Ireland is about to revolve once again on her own axis.

We shall no longer have anyone but ourselves to blame if we fail to use the freedom we have won to achieve full freedom. We are now on the natural and inevitable road to complete the work of Davis and Rooney, to restore our native tongue, to get back our history, to take up again and complete the education of our countrymen in the North-East in the national ideal, to renew our strength and refresh ourselves in our own Irish civilization, to become again the Irish men and Irish women of the distinctive Irish nation, to make real the freedom which Davis sang of, which Rooney worked for, which Tom Clarke and Seán Mac-Dermott and their comrades fought and died for.

The British have given up their claim to dominate us. They have no longer any power to prevent us making real our freedom. The complete fulfilment of our full national freedom can, however, only be won when we are "fit and willing" to win it.

Can we claim that we are yet fit and willing? Is not our country still filled with men and women who are unfit and unwilling? Are we all yet educated to be free? Has not the greater number of us still the speech of the foreigner on our tongues? Are not even we, who are proudly calling ourselves Gaels, little more than imitation Englishmen?

But we are free to remedy these things. Complete liberty—what it stands for in our Gaelic imagination—cannot be got until we have impregnated the whole of our people with the Gaelic desire. Only then shall we be worthy of the fullest freedom.

The bold outline of freedom has been drawn by the glorious efforts of the last five years; only the details remain to be filled in. Will not those who co-operated in the conception and work of the masterpiece help with the finishing touches? Can we not see that the little we have not yet gained is the expression of the falling short of our fitness for freedom? When we make ourselves fit we shall be free. If we could accept that truth we would be inspired again with the same fervour and devotion by our own "grim resolve" within the nation to complete the work which is so nearly done.

Also available from Roberts Rinehart Publishers

A New Ireland: Politics, Peace and Reconciliation
John Hume

$21.95 hardcover
Introduction by Tom McEnery and Jack Van Zandt

A New Ireland is John Hume's remarkable story of his personal struggle for recognition of his Nationalist community's rights, as well as his unending quest for peace and prosperity for all the people of Ireland.

Hume reveals for the first time the inside story of his discussions with Gerry Adams, which led to the Irish Peace Initiative and the current ceasefire. He chronicles the evolution of the Downing Street Declaration and the formation of the pan-Nationalist approach of the SDLP, Sinn Féin and the Irish government towards the peace process with Britain.

Mr. Hume's very important penultimate chapter concerns his vision of the democratic future of a united Ireland at peace.

Hume concludes by addressing the American people, and relates his unique idea for uniting people of Irish heritage throughout the world in forming an international Irish nation.

*The Troubles: Ireland's Ordeal 1966–1995 and the
Search for Peace*
Tim Pat Coogan

$29.95 hardcover

Tim Pat Coogan is one of the few journalists and writers who actually influences political events as well as writing about them. His study of the IRA and his biographies of Michael Collins and Eamon de Valera are highly controversial and definitive. This is his most important book to date: a study of the Troubles in Ireland from 1966 to the present day and beyond. He is in a unique position to write it as the most authoritative observer of the Nationalist cause, with strong political contacts on both sides of the border.

This history of what Coogan persuasively argues as the unfinished business of the north is in fact a much broader and deeper conflict, involving the politics of Britain, Ireland and America, intractable constitutional issues, and two cultures dating back to the sixteenth century and beyond. Using never-before published information, Tim Pat Coogan leads us through a complex and often devious story and assesses realistically and with inside knowledge the new possibilities for lasting peace in Ireland.

135

Michael Collins: The Man Who Made Ireland
Tim Pat Coogan

$24.95 hardcover, $14.95 paperback

'Superb...this will be a hard Life to beat.' *The Times Literary Supplement*

'Thanks to *The Man Who Made Ireland*, readers here can get the full story of this good-humoured patriot...[a] heroic account.' *The New York Times Book Review*

The IRA: A History
Tim Pat Coogan

$27.95 hardcover, $16.95 paperback

'...the standard reference work on the subject...' *The New York Times*

'No student of Irish history can afford to ignore this book. No scholar is likely to improve upon it...A fascinating book, of the greatest possible value to us all.' *The Times Literary Supplement*

The Easter Rebellion: Dublin 1916
Max Caulfield

$16.95 paperback
Second Edition

First published in 1964, *The Easter Rebellion* quickly established itself as the outstanding narrative history of the 1916 Rising in Ireland. It is a scrupulously researched and superbly written account of the events of that fateful week, and provides an objective and exciting appraisal of what was perhaps the most decisive week in the making of modern Ireland.

Since Caulfield first wrote *The Easter Rebellion*, no other historian has attempted a comparable work. Caulfield's book still stands alone as the outstanding survey of the subject.

Guerilla Days in Ireland: A Personal Account of the Anglo-Irish War
Tom Barry

$12.95 paperback
Second Edition

Seven weeks before the truce to the Anglo-Irish War of July, 1921, the British presence in County Cork consisted of over 12,500 men. Against these British forces stood the Irish Republican Army whose "Flying Columns" never exceeded 310 riflemen in the whole of County Cork, men with "no experience of war".

Guerilla Days in Ireland is the extraordinary story of the fight between two unequal forces, which ended in the withdrawal of the British from the twenty-six counties. In particular, it is the story of the West Cork Flying Column under Tom Barry, commander of genius and national hero.

The Course of Irish History
T.W. Moody & F.X. Martin

$16.95 paperback

Authoritative and fair-minded, this book has proven to be extremely popular for casual readers with an interest in history and Irish affairs. Now updated to reach the ceasefire of 1994 in Northern Ireland, it has served as a core text on history in Irish schools. Considered the definitive history among the Irish themselves, it is essential reading for anyone interested in the history of Ireland.

Miscarriage of Justice
Anne Maguire with Jim Gallagher

$10.95 paperback
Introduction by Elizabeth Shannon

In December 1974, Paddy and Anne Maguire, her brother, and two teenage sons were arrested on suspicion of manufacturing bombs for the IRA based on 'confessions' made by her nephew Gerard Conlon and his friend Paul Hill. The Maguires were subjected to intense interrogation and torture by the police for a week without being allowed to consult a lawyer. Tried and convicted without any acceptable evidence, Anne endured eight years in a maximum security prison; the family would not be together again for eleven years.

The popular movie *In the Name of the Father* told the story of the Guildford Four and Maguire Seven. This stirring personal account documents Anne's own story of those events, her thoughts and feelings throughout the twenty-year ordeal.

Free Ireland: Towards a Lasting Peace
Gerry Adams

$11.95 paperback

Adams' personal statement on the meaning, importance and inspiration of modern Irish republicanism.

'One corrective...to the flow of misinformation that passes for journalistic analysis of affairs in the North of Ireland, both in Britain and the Republic.' *New Statesman*

Falls Memories: A Belfast Life
Gerry Adams

$10.95 paperback

This nostalgic and very personal account of a working-class Irish community abounds with light-hearted humour.

'An interesting and indeed important addition to the understanding of the ingredients that coalesced to lead to the long years of violence in this part of the world.' *The Derry Journal*

To order any of the above please call the toll free number or order from the address below. Send payment with order (check, VISA, Mastercard) and include $3 for postage and handling for each order.

Roberts Rinehart publishes a number of titles of Irish interest. To receive further information and to be put on our mailing list, please write to us or telephone the toll free number below.

Roberts Rinehart Publishers
5455 Spine Road, Mezzanine West
Boulder, Colorado 80301

1 800 352 1985